A Book of Remembrance #1

The Jesus Movement

Then they that feared
the LORD SPOKE often
one to another: and
the LORD hearkened,
and heard it, and

a BOOK of REMEMBRANCE

was written before Him
for them that feared the LORD
and THOUGHT
upon His name.

Malachi 3:16

J. M. Rothwell

Dedication

Thanks to the risen Lord Jesus Christ who died for my sin!
Thank you to all whom have my name written in their
"Book of REMEMBERANCE"
1950 - The "Good News Club" lady Ashland, OR.
1952 - Leslie talked of Jesus when I visited her
1954 - Linda took me to church with Mrs. White
1955 - Barbara took me to church.
1962 – Priscilla became a Christian, I was there!
1966 - Floyd and Becky, Jim and Sue, meals shared
1966 – Edith teaching God's Word
1967 - Bill Birch, a visiting Pastor
I BECAME A CHRISTIAN
Thank you
J. Vernon McGee
Chuck Smith
Chuck Missler
and most of all
My Husband Merle
along with many other Biblical teachers
That fed me the Word
Thanks to the ones that allowed me to
share my faith with them,
as they are now written in my
"Book of REMEMBERANCE"
Thank you Marc Evans for patient editing
Forever thankful,
J. M. Rothwell

Table of Contents

Preface

In 1974 our family moved to Merle's hometown in Kansas. After settling in the Midwest we began to talk with our family and neighbors, about the events that changed our lives while living in Southern California amongst, the Jesus Movement revival. Our becoming "Born Again" believers, change of life goals, and the events of sharing our faith. Reading and learning from verse by verse Bible teachers of that day, were all part of the process.

I was never a student of writing. At Calvary Chapel Bible College in 1993-95. I began scratching down notes of Remembrance. Many of our fellow students were children of the Jesus Movement converts. We were encouraged to write down these ageless events of sharing our faith with results (good and bad).

Our first printing of unedited plastic bound books was given freely to friends and family. It was received by some as they made attempts to share their claims of Christ more freely. It is amazing how much a simple testimony can encourage faith and repentance.

We appreciate the work of Marc Evans revived teaching skills to edit and teach me how to make paragraphs and clarify my thoughts.

J. M. Rothwell

Introduction

This Book was not written as a personal testimony but rather to provoke the reader to allow the Holy Spirit to use His words and the proof of a changed life to influence the people in your midst as they read their Bibles and consider the claims of Christ.

As it says in the Bible we all have a book in Heaven where our stories of sharing faith with others are stored. Malachi 3:16,

God loves people, and he uses people to reach people. How will they know without a preacher?

God has given every believer "the measure of faith" Romans 12:3, (KJV).

Let's remember that eternal life is of greater importance that any other thing we can invest in. Our testimony, our time, matters.

Chapter 1
REPRODUCING FAITH

That which is born of the flesh is flesh; and
That which is born of the Spirit is spirit.
John 3:6

Many examples of reproducing faith are remembered from our life's journey during the days of the early "Jesus Movement." It seemed so easy back in the 1970's to share our faith with others. The young adults then were concerned about the Viet Nam War, The first war to ever be fought nightly on television. We could watch live coverage of our soldiers being killed or wounded each evening. The fear and pain of war made everyone feel vulnerable. This time of trouble made hearts like ground plowed for planting. Christians were given the Word to plant. As God's gardeners, planting the word of God and watching it sprout seemed easy. We pasted bumper stickers on our cars and carried our Bible, becoming visible to anyone interested in our hope of eternal life. Looking back, God used simple attempts to share personal faith with others; some confessions of faith seemed to "take," while others fell on stony ground never to mature into adult Christians.

Being a witness was our instruction from the Lord. Sorting the true believers from the false was the job God gave the angels for the end times.

Children reproduce faith naturally

Children can be our teachers reproducing faith on the earth. I reflect how Tracy, our daughter, was a child devoted to her favorite doll. It was not the best quality, so it had lost all its hair. She used this doll as a "stand in" until that day when she would have her very own child to love and care for. Being a much focused individual, she made the bearing of a child her peak experience of life.

At the age of seven, Tracy and her friend Jennifer were found kneeling at the side of her bed. When I entered the room, she perked up to report, "Jennifer just asked Jesus into her heart!" Reproducing is instinctive, spiritually as well as physically.

Missed opportunities

God is patient, as He prepares us to become His vessels to reproduce faith on the earth. As problems plow the ground of our world, we are given gifts to plant Jesus. If we don't plant, will we have a harvest? If we get too busy to share our faith, will others around us hear and become "Born Again" spiritually? God waits for us to respond to Him before He can use us to win a soul.   Often we visit with people without thinking about their spiritual needs. Patty, a friendly, 38-year-old, told a story of buying a T-Shirt that was a "classic." It said, "My life was so busy, I forgot to have children." Do we forget to witness to the people God places in our paths?

Mary, a single women in her late 30's, was one of the members on our tour group to Israel. Sitting on a wall at the top of Masada and peering over the side of the mountain, we began to visit. I spoke about my three daughters in Kansas and the recent death of our adopted son Scott. At that very moment, I was expecting the birth of my tenth grandchild. Mary spoke of her life as a college student at Berkeley years ago and criticized those that came to school to find a husband. She said, "Maybe that wasn't so dumb after all. I have a career, love my cats, but don't have children."

How these evaluations of purpose seem to compare with of many Christians these days. When I talk about the years God blessed us with the boldness to win converts, a faithful church member would say, "I never prayed that prayer with anyone."

Gospel responders are like relatives

A soul won to Christ becomes related forever beyond the limits of this world. The physical examples of life offer understanding of the perpetual style of multiplying God's family. All Christians are a product of someone sharing their relationship with Jesus. The fruits of our relationship with the Lord; love – joy – peace –gentleness - meekness and faith draw others to the true source of life, Jesus Christ.

New Christians, need nurturing, teaching, care and patience. These are characteristics experienced with child rearing. They are every Christian's responsibility.

The stories shared are not intended to be a "*How To*" manual. The intent is to draw you to your knees, yielding yourself to Jesus. Ask Him to give you the boldness to be a witness and words to witness, as you encounter the one God has placed in your path. The children that come forth will be "blood-related" through the blood of the Lord Jesus Christ. The new converts are eternal relatives forever.

How thankful I am to experience biological children that share a dual relationship. We call them our kids, but these daughters are literally sisters in the Lord an eternal relationship, superseding that of a biological family. One basic problem with Christians exercising their gift to win souls is "spiritual birth control," that of denying Christ for people. Some say, "Oh, they wouldn't listen to me. They will think I'm pushing my religion on them." Why not let others reject Jesus for themselves? Often it's personal rejection which is feared. If we don't venture out, we will never realize this fulfilling experience of winning a soul to Christ.

> *Lord, You said we were to be witnesses.*
> *Please help us to do that!*

Chapter 2
PERSONAL REVIVAL

Return, ye backsliding children, and I will heal your backslidings. Behold, we come unto Thee; for Thou art the LORD our God.
Jeremiah 3:22

It was the decade of the 1990's, and we were a middle-aged couple ready to settle into a simple, predictable lifestyle. Merle and I were sorting out our fragmented life after resigning from many years of chaotic living as house-parents in a large, coed group-home of foster children. We were recovering from the hurts of mid-life, marital problems, and our work in youth group homes had isolated us from Christian friends years ago. After we opened a small maintenance business the future looked promising.

Seeking a new start, things began to come together. We agreed on a routine, of getting up early and reading the designated portions in the "One Year Bible (distributed by Tyndale Corp). Scripture started getting interesting again.

Next we made visits to small group meetings for more personal fellowship with others that loved church and Jesus. One small group focused on personal sharing while another a fill-in-the-blank topical study. Small groups began to encourage us as the zeal we once had for Christian life rekindled. The studies designed for new Christians woke us up to the original call in our lives-to win souls and lead the unsaved into fellowship within the body of Christ.

Returning to church fellowship

We became remorseful and longed for the time we had lost growing within our local church. It was embarrassing to return. Many of our old Christian friends approached us and made us feel welcomed, yet we felt distanced. Quietly sitting in the rear seats, we sang scripture songs then absorbed the messages returning each week.

Backsliders are different than the new Christian. They have a pause button on their life until they return to their walk with the Lord. These Christians become strong in a short period of time. Simple passages of scripture revive whole portions of Bible knowledge as watering a thirsty, wilted garden yields a faster crop.

The Holy Spirit uses anyone willing

Years ago Bible studies encouraged Christians new and old, to pray for the Holy Spirit to teach His word to each of us personally. Everyone was to minister. New converts were encouraged to share Christ, offering their limited knowledge of the Bible to others, providing opportunities for others to do the same. People don't have to be a scientist to reproduce a human life. New Christians can also reproduce a member to God's eternal family without being a Bible scholar.

The first miracle I experienced was that the Holy Spirit could even make the King James Version of the Bible understandable and edifying. Yes, the Holy Spirit, within me, understood it and revealed it to me.

Fitting back in can be frustrating.

Attending small church plants gave hope for our active role as lay ministers. The tithe would help get them started, and our revived knowledge of the Word could give us a place to reproduce again. These young pastors, "fresh out of seminary," were programmed with programs. Being led by the Spirit of God wasn't presented.

One pastor said that the early 1970's are taught in seminary to be the "Great Falling Away". Professors taught that The "Jesus Movement" preachers drew all the people out of other churches after they got them, the people, "just fell away." I had always remembered those days in Southern California as revival.

One pastor's wife didn't like Child Evangelism materials, because "they encouraged children to pray and receive Jesus." Only story telling could be done in her church Sunday school.

Our solution to this mind set was to buy stacks of "One Year Bibles" to give away in hopes that a reading program would catch on with others as it was doing for us. It was effective because we began having conversations with friends about the reading for that week. Other stagnant believers were encouraged also.

Reading books about ministry

Having lived in the Midwest for over 20 years, my love for reading led me to a book (called Harvest), written by Pastor Chuck Smith. He was our teacher for many years in California. This book had accounts of people from the early "Jesus Movement" in our midst that had become leaders in evangelism. It certainly made us feel we had "missed the boat" somewhere and landed on an island all alone. Regrets started surfacing as we became more discontented.

One Sunday our daughter Janene stopped by after church. She was the reader of the family! She seldom can pass a book without picking it up to investigate its contents. So it was this day. Her eyes scanned the coffee table and settled on a tattered book dated from the early 1950's by Billy Graham. Purchased from a used book shelf at a thrift store, Merle and I had started reading it together. The stories were about people in the middle years who dropped everything to become missionaries, changing their entire lives. She slowly glanced up from the pages and asked, "When are you leaving?"

> *Lord, You said to not forsake the*
> *Gathering of ourselves together...*
> *Where do You want us to be?*

Chapter 3
RENEWING the CALL

I have seen his ways, and will heal him:
And restore comforts unto him
And to his mourners.

Isaiah 57:18

In 1993 we were another middle-aged couple called back into active service for the Lord. The timing was perfect. Our daughter Sheila and her husband were house hunting in the country, and making our house available to her family helped us to release our grip on property, which anchored us in Kansas. We stacked personal belongings in the barn, then set out to Bible college in Southern California.

Sheila would be graduating from nursing school at the same time we would complete Bible college. Was it great timing, or just yielding to the Lords plans? It was good becoming active again and feeling the confidence that we were in God's will.

Becoming a Bible College student

Arriving in Twin Peaks CA CCBC, Merle and I were among the few older enrollees starting this Bible college.

It was wonderful to see the variety of students drawn to this school. Many displayed the various fads of our day. Everyone was different, yet all had some things in common: wanting to learn the Bible or to prepare for ministry.

The school had a condensed program of Bible learning designed to get the most possible teaching in the shortest amount of time. The enrollees seemed to be in different stages of their Christian walk. All over campus students could be seen listening to taped commentaries on the Bible or praying with others. This place was affectionately called a "Christian Disneyland." Outside distractions were kept to a minimum. Without purchasing cable, no television was available here up in the mountains near San Bernardino.

Many people here in California wore t-shirts that said "Harvest" on the back, advertising evangelistic crusades.

Another middle-aged couple we met, Kendal and Mary Lou, had careers and a home, also came to this small Bible college. This was their first semester also.

Kendal had worked on one of the Harvest crusades and told us of the thousands coming to Christ at a baseball stadium. The "Jesus Movement" church, called Calvary Chapel, had now multiplied to over 500 branch churches that taught evangelism and God's Word, world-wide.

The motivation for abandoning our lifestyle and coming to Calvary Chapel Bible College with students from many nations, lifestyles and cultures was to learn ministry, based on the teaching of the full message of the Bible.

Returning to ministry

We had asked God to help us reach out again and trust Him, having repented of sin and our neglect of service. God's Word promised to restore us. His forgiveness filled our hearts, as we prayed, "Please Jesus, give us a second chance to do ministry again."

There are many a youth won to Christ, delivered from drugs, prostitution or other social damage of these days, who become bold street ministers, more effective at evangelism than the groomed Bible student from the schools of our popular denominations.

Jesus calls the older saints, with stacked failures and missed opportunities to become flexible, confident and yielded, fit for the Masters use as soul winners. "Oh, Lord, help us encourage the backslidden and lost to come back." They will be embraced and restored by the risen Lord Jesus Christ and by the power of His Holy Spirit.

Looking back to our beginnings

Our story began during the late 1960's. Our marriage had survived Merle's tour in Vietnam and struggles to find employment. Much time was spent birthing our three daughters and buying a new home. We had become Christians, attended church, got baptized and even traveled to Oregon for a brief time, where we were encouraged by a small church with a strong ministry to young believers. The people of that church did the plowing and planting in our hearts that led us to our association with the early "Jesus Movement" in Southern California.

Everything changed for us after a deliberate prayer together asking the Lord to help us, our heading in one direction with its set of priorities. Then, by prayerful choice, in agreement, we started a new and totally different lifestyle. We had become servants to minister Jesus Christ to anyone that would listen. Many people did.

Lord You said, "For Godly sorrow works
repentance to salvation."
Were back. Now what?

Chapter 4
HOW GOD DREW US!

I sent you to reap that whereon ye bestowed no labor, Ye are entered into their labors.

John 4:38

During the fall season of 1966 Merle was newly employed at a electrical steam plant but soon became stabilized in this new job. The company was 25 years old and the founders had begun to retire, opening up opportunities for young recruits to advance quickly and fill the jobs vacated.

We lived in Lawndale, California, in a rental house placed to the rear of a lot behind our landlord's home. A carport separated the two dwellings and doubled as a covered patio when needed. During the summer the grass area along the side held a wading pool for our Janene, now thirteen months old. The sweet peas growing on the tall privacy fence along the east side of the yard had bloomed all summer and were now revealing the end of the season, as the stems wound around the weathered string began to dry.

Christian Hospitality Encourages

The landlords, Floyd and Becky, attended church every Sunday. They made it a point to keep that day free for family and fellowship. Though they were old enough to be our parents, they treated us like friends. Accepting their invitations for dinner started a tradition of sharing meals on Sunday afternoons out under the carport. Another couple from their church, Sue and Jim, came to these shared picnics. Observing the various conversations about the church service they had attended, we concluded they liked going to church!

These people taught us to pitch horseshoes, play board games, or just sit enjoy visiting with them. Floyd began conversations about different things in the Bible. They were the only Christian people close by, and we viewed their witness to us as just a "lifestyle." Floyd prayed at the meals and strived to live the faith with Merle and I as non-Christian guests in the midst of their family.

A Home Bible Study

One Saturday evening, we decided to invite a couple Doug and Sherry, over for pizza. She politely declined then said, "Sorry, but we're going to a potluck tonight and a Bible study."

"On Saturday night?" I was a little surprised. Some people went to church on Sunday. but Saturday night seemed unusual to me. The Bible topic had come up a lot lately with our landlords.

After a long silence, Sherry hesitantly asked if we would like to go with them. "It's not square or anything, lots of nice couples get together."

Merle was always interested in food, so a dinner might help encourage him to attend this meeting. I approached him saying, "They want us to go to a POT LUCK DINNER and a little Bible study." He agreed to go. The food was a great incentive.

I searched for the zipper-covered Bible received from a New Age church my family had attended during my childhood. This Bible was represented there as a religious item but reading it never was encouraged. The Church taught positive thinking, not scripture. Worn on the outside, though never opened, it went with us to this gathering, tucked under my arm.

Becky gladly offered to watch our baby. "She sure seemed excited about this plan to attend a Bible study," I mused. Perhaps she figured this would *"perk up"* the visits with Floyd when Sunday rolled around.

We arrived at a small house crowded with young couples. The group seemed to be new students of the Bible. The men gathered outside and talked about sports events as the women arranged the food on the table. Sherry was right! This group was rather nice. New people were made to feel comfortable with them. The food went fast, dishes were placed in the kitchen, then all crowded into the living room filling the seats, then the floor.

Edith, in her early 40's, taught a verse-by-verse study in the book of Esther. She made the story come alive. Everyone seemed to enjoy her message as she applied the story to modern living. This was a long Bible study. Merle cornered her after the lesson and wanted to know where a person should start if he desired to read the Bible. She suggested the book of John.

At home, after settling the baby to bed, I approached Merle who was sitting with the Bible open. He seemed puzzled. "There's four books of John," he replied, "Wonder which one she meant?" After settling with just plain John, it didn't take us long to give up on the understanding. Figuring we just weren't cut out for this Bible study stuff, we still planned to go back, "just to meet other couples!"

The following months we continued attending this group as it was hosted in a different home each Saturday night. Attending these meetings became top priority as our interest in the studies increased. We even hosted one or two. A desire to visit churches followed. We went to a Baptist church, where Edith taught the adult Sunday school. There I filled out a visitation card.

Giving a Bible and encouragement

One Saturday afternoon Merle's helped Floyd fix the transmission on his car. It was a hot July day as Merle's legs and feet stuck out the underside of the car. He whipped his shoulders to move the dolly that shifted in jerks. I was in the seventh month of pregnancy, with our second child due in October. My bleach blond hair had lost its luster as the roots had grown out a whole inch. I tried to hasten the yield to the natural color by cutting it off as short as I dared. "Wonder if a perm would help? Probably would leave me bald," I mused. While folding diapers as Janene was still napping, a man slowly passed beside the front house and the car Merle was under, and approached our rear house. Picking up some scattered toys, I went to the door to see what he wanted.

He introduced himself as pastor Bill Birch and said he was helping out with visitations. He lifted a card out of the Bible clutched in his hand. It was the one I filled out on Sunday. Offering him a chair, I went to solicit Merle, who was now standing by his project, taking a break. I called out, "Merle it's a preacher, from the church we visited!" Using a rag to remove the excess grease from his hands, he headed for the house to meet this guest.

Offering a opportunity for prayer

After a generic greeting, pastor Birch asked us if we were Christians. Merle said, "I'm Catholic."

My turn came for a response and I shrugged, "What do you mean? Are you a Christian?" I honestly didn't understand the term.

"Have you ever prayed with someone to ask Jesus into your heart?" he enquired. We both looked puzzled and said, "No." He opened his well-worn Bible and asked permission to show us a Scripture. Then he began with reading Romans 10:9-10. *"If you confess with your mouth the Lord Jesus and believe in your heart that God hath raised him from the dead, thou shalt be saved."*

Merle crossed the room to look at the words for himself. "I didn't know the Bible actually said that!" he mused. Then pastor Birch offered to pray with us "right now if you want to!" When Merle found out he needed to pray, he didn't hesitate. Feeling rather perplexed, I copied Merle as Pastor Birch requested we get on our knees. After repeating each line of the prayer Merle was silent as the pastor looked at me.

A different approach to prayer

I said, "Do I have to say I believe in Jesus?" He nodded. I regretfully responded, "So I have to LIE to God to get saved? I wish I did believe it but I don't." (Being raised in the New Age philosophies made me feel okay about myself, if I would just-relax more!) The recent Six-Day War over in Jerusalem on the news lately made some Christians at the Bible study talk of the soon return of Jesus. I feared missing this opportunity, yet I wanted to be honest and genuine.

This kind pastor offered a solution after my admission about the lying. "No one had ever ask that before!" To redeem the moment, he offered to alter this prayer for me, by using the term "IF".

So I prayed after him, "Jesus, IF You came, and died on the cross for my sin, IF You rose from the grave, IF You died for me, please come into my heart." Then I said, "If He did I would want Him to!" pastor Birch promised to pray for us then left for his next requested visit.

Merle quietly said, "Hmm. . .THAT was interesting." I agreed.

Christians reaching to the unsaved

While Merle completed his auto-repair job, I took Janene and went to tell Becky of our confessions of faith. It surprised me as she proclaimed with tears,

"OH my goodness! PRAISE THE LORD!" as she looked for a tissue, the move of God always caused tears to poor down her face.

Floyd and Becky had a profound influence on the decision of that day. They were very real to us, fit us into their busy schedule reflecting the extent of their faith, and caused us to desire to be Christians. The weekly scheduled Bible studies helped but couldn't compare with the personal offering of time and love we experienced with Floyd and Becky. When we moved away, they followed up with many visits. Years later we visited them in Missouri the week before Floyd left to be with the Lord. After a time Becky followed him. Our family eagerly looks forward to seeing them again, in Heaven

Some plant, others water, some reap in the harvest ....as God gives the increase.

Lord You said no one comes to You except the Spirit draw them...Please continue to do that.

Chapter 5
WALKING the FENCE

***A double-minded man is unstable
in all his ways.***

This promised to be a great year. Our new baby girl Sheila was four months old, and we were owners of our first house in Garden Grove, California, forty miles east of Lawndale. There was great anticipation with this move. As new believers we were still weak in the faith and were venturing away from the home Bible study and fellowships we had grown to appreciate.

Settling into the new house, little time was wasted meeting new neighbors when we discovered our little two year old Janene was missing instead of taking her nap. Neighbors streamed out to help look for her as local law enforcement drove the neighborhood. She was located a block away between two ladies attempting to find her home. "I took a walk," she proudly informed us, never understanding why people got so upset!

This incident of panic revealed the need for a closer relationship with God. I prayed for her safety, but my prayers seemed powerless, as distance kept us from attending Bible studies. The neglect of prayer and fellowship began to bother us.

Distance doesn't matter

The phone rang. "Hi, this is Edith," the cheerful voice said over the line. "I've been praying about having a woman's Bible study in your area and wondered if you would let us use your home."

It was hard to believe she would consider a forty-mile trip each week just to have a Bible study, but she did. It seemed like most of the people who attended arrived in her car. Looking back, it was the awesome hand of God drawing me to Him through the study of His word. Edith was truly a faithful servant.

Teaching the book of John verse by verse, then Geneses, she was faithful to come every Tuesday for over two years. This group of ladies was a blessing through the pregnancy and birth of our third daughter, Tracy. The group also grew as some of the local neighbors came as well. Merle worked evening shift, so cleaning house at night while listening to J. Vernon McGee on the radio taught me more Scripture. As God answered the prayers for understanding of His Word.

Social distractions cause backsliding

We were walking the fence and still uncommitted when a neighbor encouraged me to join the Jr. Woman's Club of Garden Grove. It was a civic-minded group that hosted charity events but majored in social gatherings consisting of about ten couples. We attended many theme parties they planned, such as Las Vegas night, kidnap breakfasts, Halloween parties and the like. They were a very active group. Keeping up with this social life became addictive; it also ran us over spiritually.

The smoking habit needs to go

Smoking didn't bother me until becoming a Christian. Realizing the difficulty of dropping the habit, Edith encouraged me to focus on the Lord. She said, "It's like the leafing of a tree, as the new life flows in, the old just sheds itself naturally." She then promised to pray for me.

Each morning, our girls watched a new program on television called "Sesame Street." New anti-smoking commercials had started running with one showing a women pulled over by a law officer. She turned to look at him, as her cigarette crushed and broke against the closed window. A warning flashed, "STOP SMOKING!"

We wanted Janene now five years old to learn God's Word, so she attended a Vacation Bible School. We had neglected our faith, but wanted her to get understanding early in life. She loved it, but came home very concerned about us, asking us to go to church again.

One night, after kissing the children good-night and warning them to go right to sleep, the usual mumbling was going on. Quietly approaching the door to monitor them, Janene was heard saying, "Dear God, please take cigarettes away from my Mommy and Daddy. I don't want them to die!" Three-year-old Sheila said, "Yeah! and don't let them throw my Mommy in jail! AMEN." I peaked around the corner to find them both on their knees. I just sat on the floor of the hall and cried.

The Lord must have been dealing with Merle also as he seemed to get more and more uncomfortable with our social life. It was so confusing to drink beer while talking about the Bible to friends.

Prayers and Baptism, have power

The struggle stopped the night Merle coaxed me to my knees with him for prayer. He then asked God to help us. His prayer was so simple yet had a huge impact on the future.

We decided the following day to sell our house and move to Oregon. Determined to do all that the Bible said to do, we looked for a place to be baptized before moving. We called a church in the phone book listed as "Baptist," and the minister said he could baptize us. We gave our testimony to their board and they agreed to perform the ceremony though we didn't plan to join their church.

Our house sold fast. With the pickup and small trailer packed our family moved north, desiring to start a new life as Christians. It had been three years since the prayers to receive Jesus; Now we were getting up and starting to walk that walk. It was amazing how the Lord began to lead and teach us so much in such a short period of time. We had Jesus; now He had us. We had made a clear decision there would be no more fence walking for us!

Lord, You said You would rather we were cold or hot. We don't like lukewarm either!

Chapter 6
The GREENHOUSE

As newborn babes, desire the sincere milk of the word, that ye may grow thereby:
1 Peter 2:2

This trip to Oregon was like living in a greenhouse, being filled with seeds of God's Word. We were warmed with love, watered with gentle caring, and pruned of worldly hang-ups, however we returned to California in just four months. God sent us there, as His finishing school to prepare us for the things He had planned for us to do.

The Baptist church close by was located less than a block from our rented town-house in Aloha, Oregon. Recently the pastor and his wife had been touched by the baptism of the Holy Spirit.

Apparently, not all the members there agreed with the scriptures about the Holy Spirit's offer to believers. Comments about "private prayer meetings" were overheard.

The first service we attended, the people received us as long lost relatives attending a family reunion.

Being Hugged, fed, and visited by these church members daily for four months hastened the changes needed to make our hearts more Christ-like.

Church visits help change

Pastor Leo came over the first week with new Bibles and a welcome to his church. Confessing our inability to stop smoking, Merle told him how others that smoked could be used by God, "while witnessing for the Lord." Pastor Leo gently stopped our excuses, and said, "I don't know if it's the Lord's will for you to smoke or not. We can ask Him to take care of the problem, if there is one." This seemed like a good idea. With folded hands and bowed head, he began to pray, "Lord, if it's Your will for Joan and Merle to stop smoking, then I ask you to take away the desire and set them free. Amen!" He concluded his customary visit to newcomers and left. We both lit up a cigarette and agreed not to smoke around these church people.

The location of our town-house, brought frequent guests to our door. If someone had a duty at the church, many would stop by to see us.

During a break, having a cigarette was what we did to relax! Now it made us nervous. Newly-lighted cigarettes were frequently crushed out as we opened the door to friendly faces from this little Baptist church. After a couple days of this, we both realized, we had lost our desire for smoking!

The speaking in tongues question

Randy had pockets full of candy and a trail of little ones following him around. He gave his heart and time to the youth, then fixed appliances all around the community. His wife Marcia sang opera professionally and delighted our humble fellowship as she filled the church with a solo offering, singing without the need of a microphone.

One Sunday evening, we were invited along with many others to their house after church. They all gathered around to pray. As some people mumbled prayers that I didn't understand, I began to wonder if these might be "Pentecostal" types. Merle and Floyd had talked a little about the "tongues" Scriptures.

Worship with raised hands

There was another concern about this church. Some people there raised their hands when they sang. I wondered if they expected me to do that! As the Lord read my heart, He sent a girl, blind from birth, to become a friend. She spent lots of time at my house when Merle was working. During most of our conversation in the daytime, she would gently raise her hand toward the sliding glass door. She also did this a lot outside. When asked why she talked with her hand extended upwards, she joyfully said, "Oh, it's just a habit. I feel the heat of the sun on my palm." It may not relate to everyone, but raising hands to worship the "SON" never again was a problem for me. Jesus often has poured the warmth of His love into me that way.

The Baptism of the Holy Spirit

The children were in bed early, as Merle walked over to the men's prayer meeting at the church. This night I waited up for him. Lately, I had been evaluating the changes in my life's priority list. Asking Jesus into my heart, getting baptized, going to Bible studies, and now, experiencing miracles like losing the desire to smoke were all part of the miraculous transition. Just then, Merle came in the door smiling, "Joan, the men prayed for me tonight! I think I felt the Holy Spirit."

Renewing Marriage Vows

On our 6th wedding anniversary. Pastor Leo and Ernestine approached us, with a special invitation. They had conducted a wedding that day and still had flowers around. They wondered if we would like to say our wedding vows over and then dedicate the rest of our marriage to the Lord tonight at the church.

It was hard saying our marital vows. The eyes are the windows of the soul, so our eye contact revealed the hidden hurts and things collected there. The private ceremony that night left a real impact on both of us. Our relationship got a new start and a fresh hope, as they prayed for us and our future. We thank the Lord for them each time that service comes to mind.

> *Lord You said You would complete the work*
> *You started in us.*
> *How long will it take?*

Chapter 7
A HOUSE MINISTRY

A new commandment I give unto you,
That ye love one another; as I have loved you,
John 13:34

Randy picked up Merle to check a washer repair job at a large old house on the highway. He returned with a report, "Both guys and girls live there together, and they're Christians! They hold Bible studies and everything Joan." I had seen different "street people" going in that house while walking the children. These guys had long hair and wore overhauls. I'd never seen a Christian that looked like that before.

We needed a baby sitter, so Randy suggested calling this house on the corner, now known as "Shiloh" I refused his suggestion saying, "I know! They said they were Christians, but I'm not going to leave my children with any of them!"

The gift of food

Life was a struggle financially as Merle made minimum wage at the packing plant, and the second trust deed on the sale of the Garden Grove house covered only part of the rent here. It was a challenge making groceries stretch. A strict budget and good planning to insure good meals until payday still didn't work, as the refrigerator became nearly barren by the end of two weeks.

As I gazed into the crisper and wondered how to prepare the few items there. There was a knock at the door. When I opened it, two girls dressed in jeans and checkered shirts stood outside. One had long hair streaming past her shoulders. The other had hers braided, and she was holding a small box of vegetables. I thought they were selling them and prepared myself to refuse; I simply wasn't able to buy anything. They just smiled.

"Hi, we live at the Shiloh house down on the corner. Your husband came by when our washer didn't work. The Lord laid it on our hearts to share some of these vegetables with you."

"Give them to me? Why?" I peered into the box. It had green peppers, tomatoes, onions, lettuce. a little of everything. Slowly lifting the box from her arms, I invited them to come in.

Offer your testimony

They introduced themselves and asked questions. "We heard you are a Christian; so are we." The other asked how long, earnestly interested in the way God drew me to himself. "Who prayed with you?" she asked. They listened with enthusiasm, as I told them of the visitor who had walked Merle and I through the sinner's prayer that day in Lawndale, California. Trading Christian testimonies seems to overcome all perceived differences. Before leaving they invited me to attend the Bible study and prayer meeting, held on Tuesdays at their house on the corner. It sounded like a good idea! They even fixed soup and bread for those that came.

Visit different ministries

There must have been ten people come that night. They all looked like "hippies" and made me feel welcome, though I looked like the odd one in the group. Their radiant smiles touched me and their simple prayers referred to "Father God" in awesome reverence. When a young guy started reading and teaching from the Bible, he made it sound simple! I enjoyed following the verses as he talked to us about the love of God and the forgiveness we can have now that Jesus had paid the price for our sin. All we needed to do was repent and turn to God. His Holy Spirit would help us.

After visiting them, both the guys and the girls started frequenting our house. Often they brought sample boxes of produce that supplemented my meals perfectly. They said the food had been donated to them at the grocery. They volunteered to clean the store parking lot, and the produce department personnel returned the favor by leaving the less-than-perfect items out for them. Local farmers also gave them food. Yes, the young women from this house did baby sit for us. Our girls enjoyed them as some would strum a guitar, and sing gospel songs with them. All of us encouraged their frequent visits, as they talked of how they loved to witness to people.

One day some of the residents came to say good-by. The entire household was transferring to Hoyt Street in downtown Portland, one of the worst neighborhoods in that city. They were happy to move, as there would be "lots more people to witness to."

The Lord speaks to the heart

It was cold and snowing as we neared the Christmas season, and we were in the process of moving from our town home to a house. Merle woke up one morning talking of his "Strong feeling" to return to California.

"What!" I said.

He began by telling me he thought it was the Lord. "Joan, I can't explain it but we just have to go back to California, now!" Merle phoned his work place to tell his boss of his plans. Because production was slow, his boss just wished us luck. He wouldn't need replaced.

When we returned to the town home to finish packing, the phone rang "Hi, this is Bruce! Remember me? I'm at the airport in Portland. Can you pick me up?" An officer in the Air force, Merle's brother would surprise us with visits occasionally. We knew he would be by someday soon, but now?

Be flexible

The old Chevrolet truck and trailer were packed. The plan to crowd the whole family into the front seat for the 16-hour trip to Southern California had to change when Merle's older brother asked for a ride to San Francisco. Our revised plan left me with our children at the Shiloh house in Portland.

After picking up his brother at the airport, Merle added one of the boys from the Shiloh house to the truck, he then left for California. It was cold and snowing. Later, one of the guys in the house put our three daughters and I on a bus traveling south to Manhattan Beach, California.

The ones that took us to the bus station stayed until we were lined up to board the bus. They encouraged me to attend Calvary Chapel Church in Costa Mesa, California. They said the Pastor, Chuck Smith, was a terrific teacher of the Bible and that we would be "blessed!"

Lord, You said You would come into our hearts... Help us to look past our differences to see You in the hearts of others...

Chapter 8
GO WHERE HE LEADS

***But ye shall receive power, after that the Holy
Ghost is come upon you: and ye shall be
witnesses unto Me both in Jerusalem,
and in all Judea, and in Samaria,
and unto the uttermost part of the earth.***

Acts 1:8

Knowing my mother had been looking forward to
our arrival in California, I had phoned home before
leaving so that she could watch for us. At midnight
our bus pulled out of the station with the little ones
falling asleep while snuggling next to each other. The
rumble of the motor insured their slumber as the bus
rocked down the highway. Holding and gently patting
Tracy, our one year old, the whirlwind events of the
recent past were coming to mind. God sure didn't
waste any time!

The snow was becoming noticeably thicker as we
drove south through the Siskiyou Mountains. "Hope
Merle is all right in that old truck. Pulling a trailer
could be problems in this." Sleep eventually overcame
me as I contemplated this bad weather.

The pass on the border of Oregon and California had a great view of deep gorges, but this had to be the most dangerous time of year to take this road. We woke with a jolt when the driver stopped to talk with the Highway Patrol. The pass was closed and several cars were buried under the snow. The plowing would be difficult. After a couple of hours the children woke up, and others joined in as I softly sang gospel songs with them. After my children returned to sleep, I began to wonder if Merle had made it through. Knowing the Lord was with us and with him, I prayed, "Lord, please get him across the pass safely."

Merle told me later how the truck made it through the pass. He was following a flashing yellow light. Visibility had been very poor, so he and our friend from Shiloh prayed all the way across. When they arrived at the other side, they were stopped at a road block. An officer asked them, "How did you get here?" He seemed surprised, "The pass has been completely blocked!" When Merle told him of the yellow light they followed, the officer didn't know what they were talking about. (Our bus was forced to return to a nearby town until the road was opened several hours later).

Plans can change rapidly

What a relief it was to see Merle and my mother waiting as our bus rolled into the station! After greeting us, he told how the old blue Chevrolet truck barely chugged into the driveway at my parent's house and then died. It didn't appear to be repairable. Making it all the way was miraculous!

Before we could address the problem of a vehicle, the phone rang. Merle's mother was calling from Kansas. She was crying, as she let us know her husband passed away. Bruce had called her, so she knew where to find us. She insisted we fly back to Kansas that same night. The plane tickets would be waiting at the airport for us. My mother graciously offered to keep the children "for a visit." They loved being with her, so this timing was a marvel. With our bags still packed, we headed for the airport.

Try to share then wait

After the funeral services in Kansas we spent some time with Merle's brother Harold and his wife Cheryl. When Merle persisted in bringing up his Christianity, the television was turned on and our conversation was limited. Perhaps they had been warned by Bruce that we had become "Jesus people."

Needs are met miraculously

Later, Merle's mom took him aside to ask him to take her husband's truck to California. Every time she saw it she was reminded of her loss. We were amazed at the Lord's hand. This truck was a blue Chevrolet pickup, just like the one broken down in my parent's driveway Except that it was two years newer and the engine was in perfect shape. We left that night with a replacement vehicle. The Lord had taken care of our problem before we even had time to worry about it.

The Lord provided for all of our needs so beautifully as we moved back to California. Merle contacted the electric company to see if his past boss would consider rehiring him. He started work the same week. Some friends of ours offered their vacant house to rent which was listed for sale. We moved right in. We returned to the church in Manhattan Beach, we joined a couple's prayer group. One of the couples had been driving forty-five miles to a church in Costa Mesa called Calvary Chapel and invited us to join them. It looked as if the Lord had gone to a lot of trouble to get us there. We visited and loved it. Even though it was a long drive, we made the trip often to satisfy our hunger for the understanding of the Bible.

God continues to lead

God moved from other directions at the same time. One Saturday evening, some music groups from this church in Costa Mesa came to sing at my old high school in Manhattan Beach. It was a blessing hearing their music and then sharing their testimony of Jesus.

One day, a couple from church invited us to go street-witnessing with them. After praying for direction, they suggested the bowling alley as a good place to start, and we agreed, although we only planned to watch. This was not the Lord's plan, however. After we arrived, Merle noticed some teenage boys kicking a pinball machine and wandered over to talk with them. This visit ended with one of the boys sitting on a bench praying with Merle to ask Jesus into his heart. He did it right in front of his friends! Something inside told me we would never be the same after witnessing this event.

Lord, You said he who turns a sinner from the
error of his way will
save a soul from death
and cover a multitude of sins.
What a honor to be used by You
to do soul winning.

*Restore unto me the
joy of thy salvation;
and uphold me with
thy free spirit*

Then

*will I teach transgressors
thy ways, and
sinners shall be
Converted unto thee
Psalm 51:12,13*

Chapter 9
MOVING OVER

***I have showed you all things, how that so
laboring ye ought to support the weak...***

Acts 20:35

After six months of driving to church in Costa
Mesa, we began praying and looking for a house closer
to Calvary Chapel. It was a small church, so early
arrivals got the seats inside, and those who came later
often had to sit in the adjacent patio listening over a
loud speaker. When Merle began working in Long
Beach, the city of Westminster appeared to be a good
central location for our needs.

We had received so much from the Lord this past
year in learning His Word with the Holy Spirit taking
facts and adding life to it. We desired to minister as
we had been ministered to. The desire to be socially
accepted by our old friends was gone, as they began
replacing their adequate homes with more elaborate
designs in the many new housing developments
around.

A neighborhood for witness

Westminster was also the home of Lynn and Ray, and we asked them about available houses within their area, which was actually one of the older parts in town. There were only four single family homes, at this end of the block. All the other structures were apartment complexes. Our friends had a small house nestled in shrubs behind a well manicured flower garden. Across the street stood a white house with a porch which shared a driveway with a more modern place hidden behind an avocado tree.

They drove us around to spot houses for sale. Back at our friends' home, little Tracy became occupied with Lynn's many cats while Sheila wondered verbally if she could pick "just one" of the beautiful flowers in this adored garden. The mere suggestion seemed to hasten our good-byes. Janene was standing by the car waiting to go. Working our way to the car, Merle and I stopped to observe the little farmhouse next door. As we commented about it, the owner stepped out and walked toward us. Merle said, "We kind of like your house."

A house is provided

She responded, "Want to buy it? We need to move our dog kennel business, further out of town and we're urgent to sell." In no time at all we agreed on a price. Our only financial resource for the down payment was a second trust deed acquired on the home we'd sold in Garden Grove. The following day a local investor purchased it for the exact amount needed to put down payment on this large, misplaced, two-bedroom farmhouse. We were moved within a month.

Once we were unpacked and settled in, Merle discovered a sprinkler system buried under the front lawn. He was extremely curious about the source and looked for it, rain or shine, without success. Only later did we learn that our house was the original dichondra farm in the area and how very strange we seemed to the neighbors as they peered out their windows watching us hop up and down each time the probe hit a solid object under the rain-soaked grass.

While our neighbors were watching us, we observed them from our picture window as we did our own musing at this mysterious neighborhood. One spring day we noticed the arrival of a truck loaded with furniture. We wondered about our new neighbor, a young "hippie type" girl wearing blue jeans and a halter top barely able to cover her, as she hurried about getting her furnishings moved into the house. She had barely settled in when the stream of long-haired street youth began to frequent her door. I instinctively ushered my children into the back yard to protect them from the local "undesirables."

People that need the Lord

Not long after our new neighbor settled in, the activity erupted from across her shared driveway. Nightly screams came from the house followed by police cars. It hardly seemed to affect this young woman, as she sat on her porch resting as though located in the leisure homes of the south. Our picture window served as our amphitheater as we watched the drama acted out by the characters living across the street.

During a routine weeding session of Lynn's garden next door, I approached and asked her about the incident across the street. She said the man that owned the newer house was an alcoholic and frequently beat up his live-in girlfriend. His daughter was the young woman in the house next door, a single-parent with a fifteen-month-old boy.

Living in our new home took on the feeling of adventure. Our church was strong on evangelism, especially of the youth of the Southern California area. The pastor encouraged people to frequent the services without regard to the choice of clothing, or shoes. Merle and I were intrigued by the casual ways people came to church for worship. Services were held every night. Altar calls drew people from every walk of life, old or young, with humble dress or fancily attired, worshiping together.

Outside of the comfort zone

Merle had been working a rotating shift at a high-voltage sub-station in Long Beach. One evening I hired a baby sitter so I could attend church. Not wanting to go alone, I crossed the street to invite the new neighbor. We had never waved or spoken, so an invitation to church would be unexpected. As I approached her door, my instincts told me I would not complete this mission. I knocked boldly, eliminating my chance to back out. When this girl slowly opened the door, peeked out, and said "Hello?"

I spoke to her in rapid, unbroken statements. "Hi, my name is Joan. I'm your neighbor across the street. I'm planning to go to church tonight. Want to go with me?"

"No! " I don't have a baby sitter. Besides I don't have anything to wear." I was glad that was her excuse, because our church didn't even require shoes.

"They have a sitter. Come with me, you might enjoy it! I invited you so I wouldn't have to go alone." It must have worked, because she did decide to go, provided we used her car, a rumbling old MG with a long-overdue need for a muffler.

As I got into her car, I felt as though I was entering a culture of another land. My upbringing and young adult life was always in the "Neutral Zone." We tried to be flexible enough to fit into most age groups, but this ride was strange for me sitting with this barefoot girl, in her car, with peace signs and various revolutionary slogans decorating her dash. Holding a conversation was difficult as we had so little in common, but I started to learn something about her as we drove. Her name was Donna, and the little guy in the rumble seat was Greg. Her sister Judy and kids planned to move in with her soon. I would learn and much more.

As we drove, I was keenly aware that my purpose for taking her to church was to tell her about Jesus. I had seen Merle pray with a boy in a bowling alley to become a Christian. Now I had my first opportunity to influence someone to pray that prayer. It was damp and cold this Wednesday night at church, and as usual the building was full. We found a place in the outdoor patio. Donnas' bare arms and the crying of her child in the nursery nearby told me this was surely a flop. When she said, "I need to go home," I was certain my timing must have been off. I should have waited until a warmer night. If we had gotten there earlier, perhaps we could have sat inside. We went home quietly. I thanked her for driving me and went home across the street, never expecting more. "At least she wasn't mad" was my comfort. Perhaps I could talk with her another day.

A conformation and a new believer

Two days later I opened my door to a smiling Donna. "Hi," she said. "Guess what? My sister and her husband went to your church last night with me for Bible study. They liked it. And guess what else? They prayed and asked Jesus in their heart." She related how she had heard about this church and later marveled how the pastor looked like the "gentle daddy" she never had. All the young people hugging impressed her and she really fit in with her casual attire. It seemed this "come as you are" style of evangelism was working.

Donna didn't own a Bible, so we scrambled to find one she could have. This marked the beginning of several weeks of watching her sit on her porch reading it. Often we reflected how happy it made us feel to be the ones to place this Bible in the hands of a sincere person. As she searched the Word, many questions brought her to our door. We used our concordance and reference material to find answers as we were so new in the Word ourselves.

The joy of seeing new life in Christ

One Saturday afternoon, Donna came bouncing across the street with her hands behind her back. "I have two surprises for you. One I prayed in my bath tub last night asking Jesus to come into my heart. Next I went to a swap meet today and bought you both a present." We had to wait until the curiosity was at a peak, before she revealed a large 2ft plaster bright colored crucifix. Merle and I made a rapid evaluation of choice responses. I said, "Oh thanks," as I took it in my hands. Donna left with a cheerful "Bye" and skipped off to her house. We sat for awhile trying to decide what to do with this heartfelt gift which was not really appropriate for our walls. Merle said suddenly, "I have an idea!"

He took it to the garage and sawed off the image of a man from the cross, then found shoe polish to stain the three spots where it was fastened. When we both approved, it was hung on the wall as one of our prized additions. When Donna returned later, I made her close her eyes as she entered the house. Then I related to her the wonderful news of the Gospel, how Jesus died on the cross for her sins. But, nice men took Him off the cross. Three days later He rose from the grave. "We serve a risen savior! See?"

When she opened her eyes and saw the revised cross hanging on the wall, she ran home to get the one she bought for herself, so Merle could alter it also.

By this time, her sister, Judy, became upset about all the time Donna spent across the street with us. She got mad yelling, "Get Out, GET OUT!   I'm taking the house!" Donna and little Greg's personal clothing and belongings started flying through the air onto the front lawn. It didn't take us long to decide these girls needed a break from each other. Donna spent most of her time at our house anyway, so why not just make it full time for awhile? We began picking up her things from the lawn and placing them in our home.

Children follow their parents

Little Greg seemed unshaken by this entire process. He just took it all in stride until his toys came over. When our girls started looking and touching his many possessions, the need for a more structured program became evident.

The first few days were spent organizing. It was good news to hear that Donna was a fabulous cook who loved to start the day with homemade cinnamon rolls. She also enjoyed concentrated cleaning jobs that disrupted the rest of the house for hours, but ended with the shiniest kitchen floor ever.

Everyone is changed

It was soon evident that my domestic order had changed. We didn't both fit in the kitchen, but I wasn't ready to let go. The job Donna was doing was wonderful, but I felt like I was being replaced in the domestic part of my home. I was embarrassed by my attitude, unable to recognize that God had set me free to do more study and outreach. I was so focused on the immediate that I couldn't see the overall plan from

God's perspective. Merle went to church to get counseling. We invited the person running a Christian Co-ed household called "Philadelphia House" over to help us get on the right track.

Changing our personal appearance

Our next focus was on the dress code. It was certain that Donna needed to work on her wardrobe, which was minimal at best. It seemed the Lord went before us, because she had purchased the cloth to sew up her new clothes. When they started coming together they looked like prairie dresses. With her shoulder length, naturally curly hair and the many hours in Gods' Word, she had a radiance. Our old friends commented how "angelic" she seemed. Donna was our first direct experience with the transforming power of the Holy Spirit in the life of a believer - the return to innocence.

The past still present

The entire neighborhood came out for a nightly reminder of her childhood environment. Screams echoed with loud slaps and broken glass, bringing the local law enforcement across the street to Donnas' father's house which he shared with June, his latest alcoholic live-in. Donna would stroll across the street to offer first aid or retreat to the kitchen to bake a cake. On his sober days, her Dad would do woodworking projects in his garage. He assembled beds to give our children more room to play.

Adjustment becomes natural

Our children enjoyed devotions. They entered into conversations with us about Jesus. I remember sharing with little Janene how "The Holy Spirit in you is the same size as the Holy Spirit in me". She became a confident prayer warrior. We didn't replace our television when it quit working. Gospel music filled our house. We organized household duty sharing. Donnas' old friends would come by. We would talk to them about Jesus. Many prayed with us.

*Lord You said the stranger that dwells with You
shall be unto You
as one born among You...
Thanks for Donna and Greg.*

Warning:
It is not safe to pick up
Hitchhikers
This account was in a
Unique time of our
History where they
Were everywhere
Picking them up was
commonplace and a
dangerous person
was not the norm.
This style ministry is not
encouraged for today

Chapter 10
The HITCHHIKER

Love ye therefore the stranger; for ye were strangers in the land of Egypt.

Deuteronomy 10:19

On a warm evening during July we took our open top Jeep to a Christian coffee house called the Fire Escape. Donna went out with us this night to drink cokes and listen to contemporary gospel songs. Encouraged by the people accepting Christ nightly at our church, we wanted to talk to more non-Christians about the claims of Christ. "Oh, no! It's nearly 11 pm!" I said as we hurried to get home.

Driving south on a main boulevard, I spotted a young hitchhiker with a large duffle bag at the side of the road.   What a great way to finish the evening by witnessing to someone. "Merle, please stop. Pick him up!" I coaxed, He hesitated.   "Come on," I said as Donna chimed in. He pulled to the side of the road allowing this boy to jump in the back of the open jeep with us and to lift his large hiking backpack behind him.

Merle drove the Jeep down the boulevard, and passed the turn to our house. "Where are you going? He asked the young traveler.

"Down to the beach to crash" he replied. I then began my normal interview with him. Jesus always asked a potential convert many questions. Perhaps this was the biblical style that I should use also. So it was this warm July evening.

Get to know a person

He introduced himself as David age seventeen, traveling from Illinois with a friend. He had gotten separated from his friend in Colorado. Tonight he stayed too long at Disneyland. This was why he was so late working his way to the beach.

Donna became very concerned about the safety of his plan. "People get hurt sleeping on these beaches," She warned.   Perhaps he would consider staying at one of the house ministries from our church called "Philadelphia House." They let people stay sometimes, and it was a much safer place for him.   He agreed to check with them to see if he could stay overnight.

The jeep rumbled to a stop. The house lights were on, so I went to the door to see if David could spend the night. Their first question was his age. Because he was only seventeen, they unfortunately declined to let him stay. They told us that their ministry had agreed with the local law enforcement only to accept people over the age of eighteen. With a little persuasion Merle agreed to take him to our home in Westminster. Merle mumbled under his breath as he turned around heading home. David accepted to stay at our house overnight. We took him home and offered him soup. Then this tired traveler reclined on the couch with his tightly packed bag by his side.

Don't be pushy

Seeking opportunities to move a conversation around to include a simple gospel statement checking a person's knowledge of Christ can be challenging. David was so hard to get into a conversation. "Do you go to church?" I asked.

"No, I'm Catholic." He replied.

I was uncomfortable continuing to ask probing questions. A lecture on our theology would be inappropriate. In desperation, I offered him some gospel tracts that he hastily put in a zipper pocket of his pack. We offered to let him stay another night, but he declined. Merle bid him good luck and dropped him off at a nearby boulevard to continue his journey.

God loves little miracles

Monday was back to routine. Several weeks had helped adjust our expanded household. Donna was very fond of our daughters, and little Greg fit in so well. During our morning devotion time, we talked about starting a Christian house ministry like the ones from our church. During this prayer time we offered our lives and two-bedroom home to the Lord.

Wednesday was Merle's day off and a beautiful day for a picnic. Anxious to leave, we took a loaf of bread and peanut butter and then loaded up in the jeep. On the way for this picnic, problems began as my favorite park was one location and Donna wanted to go to another.   Both of us were used to making plans our own way. It appeared this would be our first open disagreement. In frustration Merle stopped the open-top jeep "Hey, let's just pray!" He said.   After his simple prayer requesting for God to point us to the park of His choice, it seemed that Merle heard the answer to his prayer. Silently we all headed past our home to a distant park several miles north. After going under the newly constructed overpass of a freeway, all the kids yelled, "Look! There's David! See?" When Merle saw him standing on a ramp trying to thumb a ride, he stopped the jeep. We all called to him, "David!" He gave us a "double take," and then asked "How did you find me?" My reply "*in fun*" was

"God told us where you were."

"We're going on a picnic. Want to join us?" He obediently approached and climbed into the back with us. Later we heard how he had waited at that location for several hours, never getting a chance for a ride. He was unaware that the freeway was newly completed and that this was a seldom used ramp. Perhaps because God sent us there, or he was hungry, he submitted to our invitation without hesitation.

Donna and the kids ate and then fed the ducks at a nearby pond. While they were gone, Merle and I began a conversation with him. It had been three days since we had seen David. This meeting was more than coincidence. We felt that the Lord did want us to talk to him. He seemed more at ease this time as he began probing us. "Do you believe in reincarnation or talking to the dead?" he asked. Apparently the past few months had been very hard for him and his family. His father had died earlier this year followed by his grandmother while she was living with his family. Now his mother was dealing with her losses and trying to stabilize her three teenage sons. David, the middle son, often disagreed with his mother's younger brother. His uncle was deeply involved in "Mind Power" out of the lower Chicago area and claimed to have contact with David's deceased grandma. Through some statements she reportedly said, did *"seem"* like her, David had trouble believing these reported meetings. He and his uncle argued causing his mother more stress. David felt a trip across country could give him "time to think." After high school graduation he eased his Mom's reluctance by traveling with a friend. In Colorado they separated, so David continued west, hitchhiking alone.

We listened to the events following his last stay at our house. Some people at the beach had let him stay with them two nights. This day he was on his way north to an unplanned destination. We had interrupted these flexible plans for this picnic, and now the day was nearly over. Merle invited him to our house for a Bar-B-Q and more time for conversation. It was getting late, so the food sounded good to all of us as the peanut butter and jelly had been eaten hours ago. Off we went the eight miles back to our house with our new passenger. This night David was back on the couch again.

Be willing to offer little or much

The next morning he didn't seem as anxious to travel on. When evening came, he returned from church with more questions. Raised in a Catholic school David had no knowledge of the Bible. He sat with Merle and talked at length regarding a personal relationship with Jesus Christ and how the Bible talks about this. Merle told of our conversion to Christian life and then offered him a Bible to read. The following evening David went to "evangelism night "at Calvary Chapel. The moment came when he made a decision to become a Christian as well.

It seemed practical for him to stay with us. He wanted to go to more services at this unusual church that taught the Bible. Merle told him he was welcome at our house, provided he called his mother and got her permission. "She'll just tell me to come home." he said. We wanted him to stay. If it was God's will, it could stand the test.   When he called her, she surprised him by telling him to stay with us for a while. She had worried about his safety, but now she was relieved.

David called his mom on occasion and would write her often. He sent Scriptures and various literature to her. She finally prayed for Jesus to come into her life. Then discovered a friend at her work was a Christian also, and began praying with her.

Prayer moves the speed of light

Once his mom wrote to tell of a bar-B-Q planned at her home. David's uncle was coming and bringing someone to show "Mind Power" techniques. At the approximate time for her dinner in Illinois, Merle, David, Donna and I stopped and prayed. We asked the Holy Spirit to stop any spiritual things that were not of Him. Later his mom said a nun came to her meal. David's uncle was upset because these 'Mind Power' techniques "didn't work." He blamed their failure on the presents of the nun and went shopping at the department store across the street. We knew it was a result of our prayer in southern California reaching them just south of Chicago in simple answer to prayer.

Late in December, Merle asked David how he felt about returning to his home. He said he had been praying about going to Illinois. After he purchased a bus ticket, we all stood around trying to figure out how to say, "Good-bye." David faced Merle at the door and said, "You have something I want to take with me." Then he eyed Merle's favorite Bible. Merle handed it to him with a grin and a hug. Six months had gone so fast. David had never complained about sleeping on the couch the whole time. The following day the phone rang. It was David's mom. We told her he was coming home, as a surprise. She cried, "Oh! I prayed for him to come home.   I need him here now." She was so blessed to find the Lord had answered her request at the time she and her friend prayed.

Lord You said that the eyes of our
understanding would be opened...
Thanks for teaching
David so much so fast.

Chapter 11
SUFFER the CHILDREN

Suffer the little children to come unto Me, and
forbid them not: for of such is
the kingdom of God.
Mark 10:14

Children enjoy animals. We wanted more activities for Greg and our daughters. Like their parents, they enjoyed adventure. Merle took the kids on trips to feed stores to pick up farm animals. These chickens and ducks filled the kennel pens that had once housed the dogs of the previous owners. All the animals got names as the children enjoyed collecting eggs each day from Henrietta the chicken. Hatching out baby animals was fun too.

Doing these chores gave the illusion we were out in the country though our "mini farm" was contained on two lots surrounded by high privacy fences. The neighbors discovered this farm activity when a cute baby chicken became an early morning alarm clock for the densely populated apartment complexes. Afraid of annoying the neighbors we selected our pets more carefully.

The yard still had room. I planted a garden of radishes, squash and any plant that could yield a sure crop in the shortest amount of time. Then I finished the edge with a mixture of cut flower seeds. These flowers later became a ministry tool blessing the neighbors.

Janene was in kindergarten. When her teacher learned of our collection of farm pets, she came to see. At her request we provided a rabbit and a Bantu hen for her class as a "hands on" project. Though this location provided many opportunities to meet people, it was not the most desirable neighborhood for our children to play without careful supervision.

Tracy kept busy playing with Greg as Janene and Sheila were expanding their social lives outside our yard. The children at the apartments began visiting our house. Most of the parents worked, and we felt the need to monitor their play. Obvious differences in moral standards became apparent.

Our first attempts sharing the gospel (my focus) had been on the youth disillusioned by the war in Vietnam, neighbors or Merle's work associates. Now we were forced to consider these souls housed in mischievous young bodies greatly in need of supervision. Their vocabulary reflected the frustrations of their parents. Things they said caused us to conclude some of their family members had drug problems. unmarried parent figures were common-place.

Children need the Lord

In my childhood memories I had gone to a "Good News Club" in Ashland, Oregon. Because it was located in a home near my school, my mother had allowed me to go with a friend. I remembered the flannel graph stories and the kind lady that taught them. This club became my earliest exposure to the gospel message of Christ. Now at age twenty-six a new Christian unskilled in the Word, I decided to become a teacher of a neighborhood Good News Club. This could help me learn the basic Bible stories and apply them to my own life. I could teach them to my children and their friends.

This Bible club could be a tool to win children to Christ. Perhaps this was a practical solution to a growing concern about our daughter's playmates. I attended classes for Child Evangelism Association at a local church. To my delight every story offered a salvation message. It was fun making an attendance program with charts, stars and prizes. Donna cooked up irresistible treats. The children liked the idea of a club. The treats were a big incentive to draw them.

Tuesday afternoons became the talk of the neighborhood. The attendance program encouraged bringing friends. Strong gospel messages were in every lesson. These stories ministered to ages from 4-12 all in the same room. Each week an invitation to receive Jesus as personal Lord and Savior finished our lesson. First only a few children responded to this life-giving commitment. Then it became a social status, "Are you a Christian, yet?"

Vicki was only eight years old. She had frequented our home. Usually outspoken, she was one of my motivations to change our children's social environment. Vicki was the leader of the neighborhood kids. She usually directed the activities at the apartment complexes. Now she was on the outside as Tuesdays rolled around. A social jealousy became evident as Vicki stood at the opening of our sidewalk next to the sign in the yard advertising our club. She was very upset. She hunched over, threw her elbows back, and yelled, "You stupid! BIG babies! Going to church?" Some kids hesitated in making a decision between Good News Club and Vicki.

The group had grown to between 30 and 40 in our large living room. Vicki became the object of our prayers' each meeting. One day she came to me and said "My Mom's a Christian!" I told her how happy I was to hear this.

"How do you know?" I asked.

Vicki smiled and said, "Last weekend she went to see The Godfather at the movies!" During a time of reflection, I discovered not one of these children had exposure to church or a Christian family life. We started realizing God's wisdom. It was clear He placed us here. It was a privilege touching the lives of these drawn to our house. Hospitality is a gift with a blessing.

The day came that Vicki had lost control of her following. She became touched by the joy and commitment these kids had to Good News Club. She heard the club was praying for her and decided to come "Just once!"

The story I taught was about Elijah running from Jezebel. Scared on a mountain, he was hiding in a cave. *The wind came, God was not in the wind. Earthquakes, Still God was not speaking. When God responded to Elijah he spoke with a still, small voice.*

Vicki was in class this day, and deeply involved at the plight of Elijah. Perhaps she had been lonely or afraid. How wonderful it is to hear that when a person receives God's Son Jesus into her heart the power of the Holy Spirit comforts, heals, teaches, leads and calms her fears. "We are never alone!" At the end of the lesson all received an invitation to accept Jesus. Vicki stood up, walked to the flannel board, and then asked if I would pray with her. She knew all her friends were watching. She prayed as tears poured down her cheeks. The other children hugged her. What a blessing to be an instrument of God's Salvation Plan! Joy is an emotion hard to describe.

Our attendance program became more sophisticated. I'd record their birthdays and mom's first names. When a child missed our weekly meetings, I used their absence for an opportunity to visit their home and meet their parents.

These Bible stories gave me a burning desire to win souls, now that these children had accepted Christ. My next opportunity was to help their parents learn the saving knowledge of Jesus. This was a good way to continue working in the lives of Gods News converts. Christian parents were what they needed next!

Making a excuse to visit

Donna was home for our kids. She loved to be in the kitchen. Merle often worked nights or slept days. I would find convenient times to visit the absentee club members.

Johnny had only attended twice. After he had missed several sessions, I chose to visit him at home. It was dusk and as I searched the apartment numbers, I found that his apartment was to the rear of the complexes above some garages. My natural instincts told me this was not a good place to be after dark, but an inward confidence seemed to draw me. My life was in God's hands and a prayer for His protection led me on. I knocked on the door, unawares God was about to give me a progress report on my Christian walk. I could see how he was changing people around me though I was unsure about my own progress.

My knock on the door was answered quickly, Apparently this petite lady with long black hair and a knit top revealing a tattoo on her shoulder had been expecting someone else. I introduced myself as the lady with the Good News Club over on Cedar Street. "Your son Johnny had come." I told her.   Then I explained to her how I used his absence as an excuse to visit.

She introduced herself as Carol, offered me a chair at her kitchen table and then served me a cup of tea. "Wow! This is easy I thought, settling into a chair. Visually surveying her apartment, I noticed a baby sleeping on the floor with the unfolded laundry. Carol told me Johnny was due to return soon.

She began explaining to me a problem she was having with their pet boa constrictor that was seven feet in length.   It had been irritable lately and had bitten the head off their pet chicken. She said, "I let it out of the cage for exercise. Now it's lost in this apartment!"   Johnny had gone to fetch Carol's boyfriend Butch to continue the search.

I had a phobia of snakes or things that moved like them. Though this is a common phobia mine fell in the extreme category. Thoughts of snakes always gripped me with fear.

Instantly I did a quick check on my emotions. To my amazement there was no fear. A miracle had happened inside me. I felt so many fruits of the Spirit protecting my Christian witness. My flesh wanted to run home in horror, but God's Spirit took charge. Like Elijah, a still small voice gave me peace, joy and self control.

Here I sat with a cup of hot tea and a heart of hospitality while an angry Boa lay unseen in my midst. I hardly jumped when Butch, a large unshaven, tattooed "biker" filled the doorway. "Did you find it yet?" he barked. Johnny followed behind him. Carol only motioned to the back room, saying she had already checked the kitchen and living room. I could hear the careless search as Butch shifted the furniture around.

Johnny was delighted to see me. I was glad the subject changed. Perhaps I could conclude the purpose of my visit. "Johnny, we missed you at Good News Club!" I said. He gave me a minor reason for not returning then asked me to wait while he disappeared around the corner. He returned with, "Ring neck," his very own two foot long snake coiled around his arm, as he ventured toward me and cornered me at the kitchen table.

Because this snake was Johnny's beloved pet, I commented on its gracefulness and told him I could see he liked it. Then I explained my discomfort, saying "Johnny, I haven't been around snakes too much, so I prefer not to hold it, this time."

Just then Butch rounded the corner. "I found it. Wanta see?" he asked. Seemed rude not to witness his find, so I followed him to the bedroom. There it was, coiled tight under the box spring, balanced on its side. It looked like a series of knots mixed in the springs. I was glad he had found it! He said he would lure it out with a mouse later. I hastened my goodbyes and left for home.

"Lord, thank You, You did it! You gave me strength in my hour of weakness. How much You have taught me tonight to trust You to be with me in my hour of distress." The memory of that evening strengthens me even to this day.

Let the children lead their friends

Our house became the hub of the neighborhood. As summer came, kids were in and out all day long. One Jewish mother down the block needed a part-time baby sitter for her children. Debbie, aged ten and Melvin, aged eight, spent much time at our house. We seemed the most likely place to leave them. She told us that she knew I taught the Bible. It would be OK for her kids to attend our club but, I was NOT to pray with them to receive Jesus as the Messiah. Debbie and Melvin frequented the house. It was hard to miss the message of Jesus the Messiah in the stories we learned on Tuesdays. One day I saw Debbie crying in the yard. I asked her what was wrong. She said she wanted to be a Christian instead of a Jew. I told her she would always be a Jew in her body. To be a Christian you are born of the Spirit into God's family, "the Church."

She said, "My friend Rosie told me the way to become a Christian." she told her to take a cotton swab and dip it into water then touch your forehead and both shoulders. Debbie said that when she did this, "Nothing happened!" I directed her to the other kids from the club. They talked with her and then they prayed with her to accept Jesus into her heart.

Perplexed, I wondered, did I betray this Jewish mother's request, by allowing her daughter to respond to God's call? We were just answering her questions! Later while cooking the evening meal, I noticed Debbie crying again, very loudly. "Debbie, what's wrong?" I inquired.

She blurted out, "I'M SO HAPPY! I'm a Christian! Then she sobbed and sobbed. My heart pounded as I saw her mom starting up our walk. She came through the door, and rushed to Debbie who was obviously in distress.

"Debbie, what's wrong?" her mom asked.

"MOM, I BECAME A CHRISTIAN. OH, I'm so happy!" I wished I was invisible. All I could do was try to explain without success. Her mom ignored me as she hurried her children out the door. She was upset but still let the kids visit. They did however begin classes at the synagogue.

The more we shared the gospel of Christ the more people responded to it. Our confidence to continue sharing with others God put in our path grew.

Lord, You said unless
we become converted
and become as little children,
we won't enter the kingdom of heaven...
I have learned so much from them.

Chapter 12
BURDENS for BUDDIES

Wherefore come out from among them, and be ye separate, saith the Lord, and touch not the unclean thing; and I will receive you,

2 Corinthians 6:17

We started attending a small Bible study held at the home of Vic and Sammie, a young couple with several small children. They were actively sharing Christ with the youth at the small community park, near their house. Steve was a local teen that responded to their personal ministry.

Because he weighed 360 pounds, Steve appeared much older than 16. He had thick whiskers that made him look as if he had a "five o'clock shadow" most of the time. He was once a part of the rough crowd that spent most of their time in the park. When he was a part of the gang, the leaders used him as their bouncer. Steve was strong, and his weight gave him extra impact when he played the bully for the leaders. These guys at the park must have been upset to lose him when he became a Christian. They tried to persuade him to return to them and their ways. When he didn't, they began teasing and mocking him. He suffered humiliation and needed lots of encouragement not to go back. Evangelism was his desired ministry. This was his motivation to continue putting himself into situations, for these guys to make him the object of their fun. During one of these encounters, they pushed him down and then laughed at his weight. Steve ran from them, feeling deeply embarrassed. "I'll never be able to face them again," he would say.

Then the problem youth

About the same time David moved home to Illinois, Vic and Sammie moved out of the neighborhood. This left Steve as a continuous guest at our home. One day he helped me dig a hole to plant a fruit tree in the back yard. First, he watched me grip the handle of the shovel with both hands and then leap on it with little progress. He then offered to relieve me of this task. Sinking the shovel into the soft dirt by shifting his weight to one foot, then he flipped the shovel filled with dirt aside with a snap of his forearm. Gripping the tree, he easily set it in the hole. As the tree grew and grew, Steve was finding his place as a Christian brother in our home.

Merle closed in the back of the garage and added a couple beds so Steve could be our new resident. His Mom was so glad we let him stay. His older brother was having problems, and her sons were not doing well at home with their father. We had him walk to continuation school to earn his graduation diploma. This was not to indicate that he was learning the essentials like math and grammar. His good attendance was a noticeable change from his past academic record. Every day he would come home and tell Donna and I about the neat present he was making Merle for his birthday. He said that the teacher gave him some one-foot square pieces of 1/8th-inch cedar. He glued them one on top of the other and then cut on an angle to form a beautiful cross to hang on the wall.

Merle's birthday finally rolled around. Steve was a nervous wreck. He had waited so long to present this gift. He had everyone gather around and then danced from one foot to another until this cross was in view. We all were amazed at the finished product. It was more quality than we had imagined. This special gift hangs on our wall even to this day.

Try printed booklets about God

With Steve encouraging us to evangelize, all of us in the house soon got a burden for the park he once helped rule. He said he used to sleep under the bushes there when he was upset at home. I started going to this place in the daytime monitoring our children on the play equipment. My pockets were full of gospel tracts just in case a young person like Steve might be there for me to talk to. As I scanned the perimeter of the playground, I noticed a young Mexican youth, sitting on a bicycle. He could have been waiting for someone as he just sat idle. I reached into my pocket and found one of my favorite booklets called "Living Water." This tract explained the need to become a Christian in such a good way. Its cartoon form with simple language made it easy to understand. So it was with this young person approximately sixteen years old. His stern facial expression, the unpopular 2-inch ring in one ear, and the piercing look when our eyes met made me think of the famous Nicky Cruz I had read about from the streets of New York. His deliberate hostile appearance naturally caused people to move away. Obviously taken off guard that I approached him with a smile and offered him a tract, he snarled, "WHAT'S THAT?" without touching it.

"It's only a little book about God, kind of fun to read. "Here you can have it." I said as I waved it toward him. I was surprised when he took it and began to read. He said he didn't believe in any of "that stuff." Yet I sensed he had softened after reading it. It talks about the God-shaped void in man's heart and how God through Jesus Christ gives us living water overflowing. Our conversation scanned the basics of becoming a Christian. I told him I had not been one that long myself. I talked to him about the church I attended called Calvary Chapel. He listened while keeping his militant personality intact.

As noon approached I concluded our conversation because I needed to take the children home for lunch.

I offered him an invitation to come to our house for lunch also. If he wished, he could follow my car home. "The people that live in my house will gladly share their meal with you," I said. Perhaps he would have declined, but another person had approached while we were talking. He said, "Can he come too?" as he motioned toward his friend.

Talk to the kids and feed them

I told him it was normal for us to make enough food for unexpected guests. "My husband is home. He'll answer your questions better than I can." They did follow me on their bikes as I slowly drove home. Merle was working on a rail fence in our front yard. He saw my car approach, and then noticed I was being followed. Our eyes met with a knowing glance. Words weren't necessary. He knew I would volunteer, "Hi Merle.   These are some people I met   in the park today." I went on to relate the succession of events that lead to these lunch quests and included the part where he was to tell them all about Jesus and to answer their questions. He had been through this before, so he just shook their hands and motioned them toward the house. Donna didn't flinch when informed two more were coming for lunch. She just added another can of tuna to the mixture and cut up more fresh tortillas to fry in the heated oil on the stove.

Later that day, Steve returned from school to find that none other than "Tony" had been to our house.

"For Lunch? I can hardly believe it!" he barked. Then he told us of Tony and his recent release from jail. Tony was arrested for hitting an old Catholic priest that used a cane! at the church across from the park. This priest had refused to let his brother keep the money from the sale of his confetti eggs out in front of the church.

Evangelizing the neighborhood was fun these days. People were so open to hear our version of Christian life. We just didn't seem to have any fears. The young people felt the love we had for them. When they removed all the knobs out of our car and left them on the seat, we took it as a hidden message to lock it! We felt that our house was not as vulnerable a target for vandalism. Steve said they all knew our car was "OFF LIMITS!"

Assist others as they learn

It was early evening one day when Steve rushed into the house. "Hey, Merle! Get ready! QUICK! I've been talking to some guys at the park. They said they would come over and let you tell them about God. Wow! This is the day! I can't wait! Hey Joan, help me set the seats just right. Here they come!" He puffed with deep breaths as he peered out the curtain in anticipation. A small group of teens were approaching the house.

We were ready to meet this great challenge. Steve opened the door before they could knock. As the youths entered, we smiled, encouraging them that they were most welcome. Steve guided them to a seat and then told Merle, "Tell them!" All eyes focused on Merle as they waited for his message. Merle paused a moment, reflecting on the times youth came to his small Kansas town causing problems. He began his attempt to relate to the audience. It's not clear what these guys expected to hear; they weren't smiling. Merle began telling them how he remembered the Kansas City boys when they came to town. Apparently this was the wrong thing to say.

They said, "WHAT? You gotta be kiddin MAN!" Then they got up, headed to the door in a line barely picking up their feet. Shut it behind them.

Poor Steve was dumbfounded and horribly disappointed. He sat in the chair, threw his hands in the air and yelled, "Kansas City boys?" Oh, man you REALLY blew it!" Merle didn't understand what he said wrong. Steve said, "YEAH, farmers in overhauls holding pitchforks. Yeah, they'll never listen to me again. What a bummer!" Merle apologized and called us together to pray for these who had seemed to reject our message for them

Lord, please help us win young people!

Chapter 13
TRACT MINISTRY

My word it shall not return unto me void, but it shall accomplish that which I please, and it shall prosper in the thing whereto I sent it.

Isaiah 55:11

Vitamins can be good supplements, but they cannot replace a proper diet. Gospel tracts are good tools for witnessing but cannot replace proper Bible-study habits. They are like little Scripture commercials designed to target a subject drawing the reader into his Bible for more spiritual food.

Before accepting Christ, I recall picking up these little short subject booklets. I found them to be helpful to strengthen my interest in the Bible. Thankful people had left them for me. I returned the effort by leaving them for others.

We purchased stacks of "Living Water" tracts, written by young guy at church named Greg Laurie. We left them with anyone or anywhere we thought someone would read them. While waiting in the doctor's office, I'd pray as I would place one on a table and then sit on the other side of the room. It was fun to see the Holy Spirit draw someone's eye to it. The individual would pick it up, read some and then quickly stash the tract into a pocket for later as I used to do.

One Sunday after church while Merle was working, the children went down for a nap. Donna offered to stay home so I could go for a walk on this beautiful sunny day. With a pocket full of tracts I headed for the park four blocks away.

Bikers for Christ

I walked the two blocks to the boulevard. As I rounded the corner, I noticed a large group of motorcycle riders standing across the sidewalk They were looking in the window of a custom bike shop where a, sign read "Closed Sunday."

My first thought was to cross the boulevard to avoid them, But the only way to the crosswalk was to pass through them. My heart pounded as I wrestled with my decision. If God had given me a desire to go this way. why change my plans because of six couples riding motorcycles? Without any more hesitation, I headed directly toward these unsuspecting bikers. I focused on the crosswalk for courage and surprised myself when I stopped in the midst of the group.

I took a tract out of my pocket and offered it to the first girl that caught my eye. "Here, would you like this little book about God?" I asked. She curled one side of her lip in disgust, then rolled her eyes, and turned away. So I looked for another with the same offer. The group seemed to groan collectively and moved away from me.

Don't get discouraged

Then, a couple walked toward me and asked about the booklet I had in my hand. Whew! "It's Just a little book that talks about becoming a Christian," I replied. "Want one?" The young woman took it.

"Are you with the Maranatha groups that sang in Long Beach?" She asked. I told her I attended the church, where most of them went. It was time I headed on to the park.

"My phone number is on the back of the booklet. Call me if you have questions. I'll answer them if I can." I added my address in case they wanted it.

Four weeks later I was removing wall paper in the entry of our home. Merle was in the dining room visiting with a neighbor. A rumbling motorcycle thundered around the corner and stopped in our driveway.

We were not expecting more company. I peered around Merle as he opened the door. After introducing themselves as the couple I had left a tract with, I immediately invited them in. The young woman introduced herself as Amy. Her husband sat quietly as she explained her reason for the visit. She told us that she was the daughter of a minister in Tennessee. Her entire life had been spent weekly on the front pew of her church, but she couldn't remember ever reading a Bible. After her high school graduation, she married her boyfriend, stuffed the new white Bible her parents gave her into a pack mounted on the back of a motorcycle, and left for California.

She said that after talking to me at the bike shop that Sunday, she returned home and read the "Living Water" tract. This caused her to search for and open the gift box that contained the new white Bible her parents had given her as a graduation gift. She told us how she had removed the cellophane around it then wondered where to start. She began by just reading the red letters. (These were the words of Jesus.) "You told me if I had questions to come over. That's why we came. I have questions." She wanted to know why Jesus killed the fig tree, among many other things. As her questions followed one after another, Merle opened his Bible and offered her simple answers. We were still new in the Word so it was a marvel to see how he located answers in the Scriptures for her. Amy and her husband stayed all evening as she moved from one question to another. Merle then encouraged them to pray, read the Bible and get into fellowship. Then they mounted their motorcycle and left.

Six months later during a routine day, I answered the phone. "HI! I'm Amy remember me?" It did take a minute to place her, but her Tennessee accent helped. She said she had searched and searched for the tract with my phone number.   "You told me if I had questions I could call you." Amy went on to tell me of her employment as a telephone operator in Long Beach. She discovered a woman working with her was a Christian. They began to study the Word together and pray. This led them to visit a nursing home as ministry. She and this friend prayed with a lady there to receive Jesus as her personal Lord and Savior. "Now this lady wants to be baptized. What should we do?"

Amy also told me her father in Tennessee was dying of cancer. Her husband was planning to take her to see him before he died. She requested prayer for him.

Now looking back, I can see the hand of the Lord moving as he drew me to the park that day. Because Amy's family was praying in Tennessee, the Spirit of God sent me to the park so I would give a message to Amy.   She must have blessed her father to see her walking for the Lord before his death.

Thank you Lord, for Amy.

Chapter 14
NO MAN KNOWS the HOUR

For the Lord Himself shall descend from heaven with a shout. . . and with the trump of God: and the dead in Christ shall rise first:

1 Thessalonians 4:16

Learning the Bible from Genesis to Revelation helps us to see the hidden messages that God knit through the Scriptures. One Example is Enoch, the man who walked with God. Enoch *"was not because God took him"* before the great world-wide flood. His disappearance reminds me of the promises in the New Testament regarding the "snatching away" of the Church, as we will "NOT BE because God took US."

Our understanding of the scriptures draws us to conclude we should always BE ready because we don't know the day or hour of this event. It does not seem we will have time to straighten out our lives at the time of His arrival. We are the bride of Christ. To be the bride that has "made herself ready" for the coming of the Lord we must have yielded ourselves to the Holy Spirit to do a work in us. This work he accomplishes by convicting us of sin. Then as we confess and repent of these sins, He will clean us from all unrighteousness (hay, wood, and stubble). When the Lord does come, He won't have much to kindle with the fire He brings on the earth. He said, "Tarry until I come." We decided to have good family communication to help each other *"tarry"* in the Lord by spending time together.

Picnics separated us from our routines, so we would plan them frequently during the warm weather. Merle would toss a ball to the children or join them on the play equipment located in the park's near-by playground. Donna and I arranged the table while waiting for the coals to heat up in the grill at little Westminster Park.

Later we began eating our feast all gathered around the table nestled in one picnic area surrounded by overgrown hedges. Suddenly a tall thin Indian guy came through the shrubs, taking a short cut across the park. He had his long straight black hair tied down with a popular head band. Donna recognized him. "Hi, Jesse, how are you doing?" They talked awhile since she had known him briefly from the neighborhood. Donna had attended school with many young people around here. She talked to him about her new life now as a Christian and then introduced us. Jesse started to continue on his way as Donna invited him to come by our house sometime. He said, "Yeah, sure " then left.

One evening while we were sharing a Bible study with a room full of people, someone knocked at the door. when I opened it, there was Jesse. As I moved aside he walked in and then scanned the room to acknowledge the people he recognized. He knew that Donna lived here with her child, but noticed Steve was here also. He must have supposed we would let him sleep here as well. "Can I *crash* here?" (Meaning sleep overnight at our house), he boldly asked. Merle told him "No" without hesitation. Jesse may have been under the influence of a drug as he had delayed responses. The refusal slowly registered in his brain as he seemed to contemplate a new approach. After folding his hands behind his head and then taking a deep breath, Jesse slumped back on the couch and proclaimed boldly, "I've been thinking about changing my religion!" Then he waited for Merle's response. We didn't sense the need for Jesse to sleep in our home; however this did seem the appropriate time to share the gospel message with him. The conversation before his arrival had been about some witnessing in the neighborhood, so it seemed as if God had sent this group an example. Here was Jesse, the object of Merle's lesson in evangelism. When asked if he came here to accept Jesus, he said, "Yeah, I will, but not until after I spend the weekend with this ah girl." He must have known that making a commitment to Jesus would interfere with his immoral plans.

Merle began to explain the basic message of the Bible. Jesus had come two thousand years ago to die on the cross for the sins of the world, including Jesse. He continued by saying when Jesus rose from the dead, He ascended into heaven. Now all Christians wait for Him to keep His promise and to come for His bride, the church. Jesse hardly blinked as he listened. His concentration was so intent that his mouth gaped open unaware. He drew closer to hear every word.

The room full of listeners drew near to hear of the last days when a trumpet will blow and the Christians will be caught up into the air. So we will ever be with the Lord." We sat silently, then somewhere in the neighborhood totally unexpected and incredibly timed, a trumpet sounded. All of us froze! After a moment we realized this wasn't the actual recorded event. Merle looked at Jesse and said, "This could have been the moment talked of in the Bible. Do you want to pray with us to become a Christian?" He just nodded his head up and down, repeated a prayer, and then left quietly.

Take youth to church and fellowships

Later in the week I planned to go to church for the Wednesday night meeting at Calvary Chapel in Costa Mesa. These meetings were evangelistic, so I ventured past the park to see if Jesse might be there. He never returned to the house so, it seemed church was the best follow up for him after his conversion. I must have been right. There he was, sitting on a park bench. I invited him to go to with me. "You can come the way you're dressed. This is a come-as-you-are kind of church, "I told him knowing he would enjoy the service. "Jesse, you're a Christian now. You will love going to meetings with others that believe.

He agreed to come if I would consider taking one of his friends along. I especially wanted Jesse to be come, hoping he might choose tonight to make a public expression of his verbal prayer earlier in the week.

Jesse climbed into the bucket seat of the jeep and then directed me around the corner. I waited patiently as he solicited his friend within a weathered little house. As they started toward the car, I recognized his companion as Tony, the boy that ate lunch at our house a few weeks earlier. I now knew him as the leader of the rough gang here.

I felt God warning me to keep silent not to spoil what He was doing with these two that He had drawn to come with me this night. My fear about the crowding became a reality when we tried to find seats. Both boys were able to fit in the center of one of the rows near the rear of the church, and I found a tight place behind them. It seemed a great place for me to pray for them. Immediately the building filled with people. First all pews, then the rest of the chairs on the side, and the aisles filled with people sitting on the floor, with the unseen overflow filling the patio outside. Lonnie was a long-haired preacher that wore blue jeans. He began to sing loudly a little out of tune as casually dressed Debbie, who was tall with long hair, strummed her guitar at his side. He then began to tell a Bible story that spoke about Samuel being dedicated to God. How God spoke to him one night: *"Samuel . . . Samuel."* Then Lonnie continued, "Samuel thought Eli was calling him." Lonnie then applied this event to the present day, relating it to this crowd of people. He invited those who needed Christ in their life to come forward to pray. Many came forward. The audience was encouraged. Then more came. He did this again until the entire front of the church filled with potential converts. Then he said that he felt the Holy Spirit wanted him to ask "one more time." My location behind these two boys caused me to pray each time for them to heed this call. Perhaps the Lord was speaking to them. The preacher refused to conclude; he called upon the Christians to pray, followed by a long uncomfortable silence. Then I observed how Tony and Jesse stood half way up then sat back down. People in front of them did stand up; then in the next row forward, a few stood. This happened consecutively from the rear of the room to the front like a wave sweeping forward from side to side drawing many to their feet. The crowd gave a collective sigh. Lonnie paused and said, "THAT, was the Holy Spirit!"

Without ever knowing the impact this event had on my passengers, I often think of that night. It seemed to affect me greatly.

Converts belong to the Lord, he knows

The next encounter I had with Jesse was about a month later. I had gone to the house of one of Janene's friends to teach a Good News Club in the apartment complex about six blocks away. Once I had mastered a story, it was easy to repeat it within the week.   As I was leaving with all my materials grasped in my arms, heading toward my car, Jesse came across the parking area of the complex. I greeted him and asked about his faith. "How are you doing?" I probed.

He said, "Not too good." He promised to stop by and see us at our house soon, but he never did. About two months later I read a small article in the newspaper stating that Jesse had been found dead wrapped in a blanket at the base of a ditch not far from our home, reportedly from a drug overdose.

Lord, is Jesse with You? When I get to heaven, I plan to look for him.

Chapter 15
From FEAR to BOLDNESS

Fear not, nor be dismayed: for the LORD God, even my God, will be with thee; He will not fail thee, nor forsake thee, until thou hast finished all the work for the service of the house of the LORD.
1 Corinthians 28:20

Merle and his work associate Vic decided to open a part-time remodeling service. It was a business decision to put a Long Beach telephone number in our Westminster home. This phone installed in the bedroom for the business kept these calls separate from the activities of our busy household.

The electric company kept Merle on a rotating shift. He was gone all night for one week every month. As a homemaker, I was available for answering the phone to take messages. Newspaper ads were placed to draw the desired extra work.

One night this phone in my bedroom woke me up from a sound sleep. I answered it expecting it to be Merle at work. At first I detected only deep breathing. The clock said 2:00 a.m. I was barely awake as I said

"Hello hello ah hello?" I asked, "Who's there?" A deep male voice came on the line, saying provocative sexual things that changed into morbid, violent statements. My hand froze the phone to my ear. Since I was half asleep, it took a moment to realize I had answered an obscene phone call. I hung up the phone, but it rang again. This person was persistent! When I laid down the receiver, I could be hear him talking through the phone. When I hung up, he called back. (Unfortunately phones didn't unplug in those days.) Sudden fear gripped me as I scrambled to stabilize my thoughts. Hastily, I put on my robe and went to the living room using our local line to call Merle at work in Long Beach. He notified a telephone company employee who unplugged our line from their office. Merle kept me on the phone for encouragement. He reminded me that the caller thought he was phoning someone in Long Beach. (Perhaps this is why the number was available). Were the previous owners harassed by this man? We were thankful he didn't call from the phone book. Perhaps he would have known my address or figured I was alone with small children.

As I settled back to bed, I began to pray. "Lord, how come I got so scared? Did I truly trust You to protect me?" Then I pondered the condition of a soul that would seek to frighten a woman alone. What caused this person to be so "messed up." Perhaps a saving knowledge of Jesus Christ could give him a clean heart and a new start. I dozed off to sleep thinking, if this ever happens again, I'll pray for him. I'll exchange some fear for evangelistic boldness.

Merle was home the following night. When the phone rang at 2:00 a.m., He answered it. The caller hung up, never to call again.

Two days later I was in the living room vacuuming the floor. Merle had just left for work. It was early afternoon, our first 4:00 p.m. to midnight shift with him out of the house. The local phone rang and I answered it with a cheerful "Hello."   The caller responded with a deliberate heavy breathing then a voice began speaking provocative statements. This time the caller had a foreign accent. Sudden fear gripped me. I could remember the other caller calling back repeatedly. This one could have my address if he had found our number in the phone book. "Pray!" I told myself. "Jesus please help me. I don't want to let You down." This man called to harass someone but reached a servant of God. Don't let my fear hinder You," Lord.

Bad experiences can train us

"Stop . . . don't say anything else! I don't know who you are, but God does. The eyes of the Lord are in every place. He is with you right now. Today you have called a Christian. God will use me to speak to you. (softly) He understands you, your loneliness, and anger. He loves you that is why He sent Jesus Christ into the world. To help you, all you need to do is pray. Ask Jesus into your heart so the power of God's Holy Spirit can come into you and cleanse you of your sin. God will make you brand new, on the inside. Perhaps this is why you have called a Christian. This is your opportunity to get help for your soul. If you want to change and turn your life around you can start with a simple prayer. Do you want me to pray with you right now?"

Caller said, "yes"

I said, "OK, repeat after me. Father, in heaven, I believe
You visited the earth in the body of the Lord Jesus Christ."

Caller repeated obediently.

I said, "Say Jesus died on the cross for my sin. He didn't stay dead. He rose from the grave!
Caller repeated (softly).

Caller- repeated

I said, "Jesus, please come into my heart."

Caller repeated

I said, "Cleanse my heart and make me brand new."

Caller – repeated this also.

I then encouraged him to get a Bible and to attend a church that taught from it. I told him to learn God's Word and that the Holy Spirit understands it and will help him. Then told how the Word of God washes us on the inside. "You are God's child now." I said

The Caller quietly said "Thank you and hung up his phone.

I hung up the phone silently. Then I leaped in the air yelling, "PRAISE THE LORD!"

Lord, You were with me that day. I knew that boldness came from You. Thanks!

Chapter 16
EAGER to SERVE

. . . be ye steadfast, unmovable, always abound-
ing in the work of the Lord, forasmuch as ye know
that your labor is not in vain in the Lord.
1 Corinthians 15:58

We had enrolled our house with a hot line ministry. Our intent was to offer emergency shelter to callers to open up new opportunities to minister.

Calls from their office began with requests to pick up different people needing a place to stay.   John looked like a clean-cut person.   Raised in an upper class family, but his parents had moved not giving him their address because his drug problem caused him to steal from them. He was their son so they wouldn't prosecute, but they chose to keep the location of home anonymous. John could only contact them through a mutual friend.   They had learned he couldn't be trusted as he offered empty promises to avoid drugs.

This young man tried hard to follow the rules we set for him. He preferred to be with others as a support for his desire to shake the drug problem. John stayed with us throughout the Thanksgiving holidays. His parents came to see him at our home. They were Christians and felt his stay at our house was an answer to their prayers. His parents were pleased that we encouraged John to attend church and listen to cassette tapes teaching the Bible. He did well until his girlfriend found out he was in a Christian house. She persuaded him to come with her. She Drove over one day and picked him up. He left knowing he could not return. We had written guidelines that an applicant had to follow. We didn't allow smoking or drugs to spoil the atmosphere we had created by playing Christian music and praying often.

Our church pastor Chuck Smith, taught a message about not trying to beat away the darkness. "Just turn on the light!" he said. This saying helped a lot as we would reach out to the lost. We were fishers of men. We caught them, and we let God cleanse them.

Normally, no individuals resided in our house until we knew them, and of their desire to change their life's direction. This decision to offer shelter to hot line callers was intended to touch more people with the message of Christ.

Some people just don't get it.

A guy named James said and did all that we could ever ask of a person. He was friendly, read his Bible, and went to church. We did not quite understand our cautions about him. He would leave and come home with gifts for the others in the house. He seemed to enjoy all the appreciation. Then one day we received a phone call from a local merchant. James was writing bad checks in the neighborhood stores, and someone had traced him to our house. We called a taxi and sent him back to the location where we picked him up. He acted unshaken. It seemed to us that this young man had done this before. Perhaps he wasn't ready for a change.

A young woman came with her two children. She chose not to stay because of the "no smoking" rule. The need for cigarettes caused her to choose a slum apartment for her family. That apartment was provided by the local social services we directed her to.

Lord, please help us with the
gift of discernment.
Sometimes were not sure of Your will.

Chapter 17
The PASTOR'S WIFE

***To the weak became I as weak, that I might
gain the weak: I am made all things to all men,
that I might by all means save some.***
1 Corinthians 9:22

We did a periodic evaluation of our personal family life. It revealed that our children were doing well. We enjoyed working with the various people that crossed our path; however we began to long for the family atmosphere we used to enjoy with others. We felt the need for exposure to the *ordinary* style of church life. Somewhere nearby we could attend a smaller fellowship with families. It would help our personal family unit become more defined. Donna started strengthening her relationship with Greg as she took him to theme parks and small trips.

Three years ago we had attended a local Christian Church when we had lived in Garden Grove. Janene had attended a vacation Bible school there that greatly influenced her as she, in turn encouraged, us to attend church. They now had a new younger pastor. The church was growing, and the emphasis had gone to evangelism and strengthening the family walk with the Lord. We could see that our wardrobes needed updating so that we would not stand out in the crowd. We chose to drop the more leisurely look and update to fit into ordinary church.

Adapt to other styles of Christians

We purchased a new outfit for each member of our family. I got a more stylish hair cut. Our first Sunday was wonderful. The pastor's message was easy to understand. The Sunday school programs were small and intimate, so our children were quick to make friends.

We grew fond of the pastor and his wife, Rich and Wilma, who both truly loved the Lord. We invited them to dinner. They came to our house and were very gracious. Wilma had a heart for service to the Lord. She was curious about our Christian walk and this ministry in our house. She seemed touched by the way lay people can do active ministry winning souls. Her curiosity and questions drew her back to our house one early evening for a visit. I wanted to become better acquainted. This opportunity to get to know her made being part of a smaller church seemed so normal.

Don't get shaken by the unexpected

Wilma's father was a minister. She had been reared in a very Godly Christian home and had met her husband at Bible college. Now that she was the wife of a pastor with a fast growing congregation, she began learning the greater complexities involved in church leadership. Wilma was curious about the Jesus movement with the Hippies and street youth coming to Christ, Mostly just young families. The basis for our friendship was our mutual interest in our different styles of service.

It was a warm summer evening with longer days, and the windows were open taking in what breeze could find us. Merle was working an evening shift this day, so my planned visit with Wilma was going to be special for me.   Donna and I were cleaning up the supper dishes as she drove up.

Our conversation was interrupted suddenly when we heard a woman scream LOUDLY! These horrible sounds were coming from across the street. We then heard the crashing furniture, then broken glass. Wilma froze in her seat. I shot a glance to the kitchen as Donna peaked her head around and looked at us. "OOPS, they're at it again!"

I tried to explain to this gentle pastor's wife about this recurring problem. How Donnas' alcoholic father lived across the street with his girlfriend. "These outbursts are continuous. Even the broken glass happens a lot," I said, attempting to make it seem normal. Then I continued, explaining to her how each time Donnas' Dad Bud and his girlfriend June get drunk their fights become violent and how they often break one of the glass pains in the front door. "Fortunately they were replacing them with Plexiglas," I said. She looked extremely disturbed by the loud noise and the violence as it escalated with the foul language. My attempts to explain didn't seem to help.

Donna strolled to the front door taking a deep breath she dreaded this reminder of her past life. I liked to monitor the involvement as a "back up" when Donna interrupted these episodes. So I invited Wilma to sit with me on the porch. My statement that the police would arrive soon didn't make her comfortable. She hastened her good-byes as I escorted her to her car parked across the street, as she had a tight hold on my arm and hand.

Visitation program

The following weeks, I was determined to pursue fellowship at this church. I taught a Sunday school class using my flannel graph materials. The following Tuesday evening I attended visitation night. Part of this program for evangelism consisted of responding to visit requests. About fifteen people got together to pray and then formed teams. Each team consisted of two or three persons and visited one or two families, concluding with a gathering at the home of a deacon. This proved to be a very effective method of contact as it reminded me of the person that had visited our house years ago, holding on to a signed card we had filled out once. I Recalled that day as a milestone in our lives as Merle and I had responded to a visiting pastor. He had lead us to the Lord with a prayer for salvation in our living room.

Later this evening the teams started arriving for refreshments and testimony of the various contacts. Some individuals had asked questions about the church while others wanted to know more about Christianity. Some of the people had personal prayer needs. This was a small group so it was easy to get to know people.   The conversations changed to the participants' different vacation plans. I started saying that my husband was talking more about going to Kansas lately. A young man across the room overheard and asked. "Who's from Kansas?" Our conversation continued as I explained how my husband had left a small town in the Midwest for the navy and had been stationed in Long Beach, where we had met and married nearly ten years ago. When I mentioned Merle was born and raised in the town of Lawrence, he replied,   "Lawrence that's where my wife and I are from." He then moved across the room and probed me for more detail. He could hardly believe it when we discovered that he knew my husband and his family. Memories of Merle flashed from childhood. "MERLE'S A CHRISTIAN?" he asked loudly, as in unbelief. Then he clasped his hand over his mouth realizing, how very loud he had said it.   We exchanged phone numbers and planned to get our families together.

Merle remembered this couple named John and Patty. They were some grades ahead of him in Lawrence High school years ago. Merle remembered them as more adapted to academic life than he. Patty was a cheer leader and John was considered popular. John's parents had partied with Merle's a lot

This brief encounter was one of those coincidences we hear about in the densely populated southern California basin. It was fun to reflect what a small world we lived in. Perhaps this meeting acted as the springboard to shift our family focus to the people Merle knew and was raised with. He began to muse about the spiritual condition of so many of them back in Kansas.

Lord, where do you want us to minister?
I love this church, but what about the Jesus
Movement converts.
We love them too.

Chapter 18
MODERN MARY MAGDALENE

*.......Jesus said unto her, Neither do I condemn
thee: go, and sin no more.*

John 8:11

After a time Donna chose to get a job and to pay a
bed and board fee. She wanted to have days outside
the house. I offered to keep Greg for her while she
worked. Her first job at a nursing center was the
beginning of her burden for the plight of physically
and mentally disabled youth that resided there. She
began taking Greg and our daughters to visit them.
They enjoyed it as a field trip.

Things started to change after Merle went to the
attic to find out how much room was up there, he
discovered that the ceiling had been lowered.   The
lumber on the old one was still in place. He went
through the hall closet then built a staircase to the
second floor. The boards cut out from the old ceiling
were usable to beef up the one below. Donnas' dad
came across the street and built in beds with fitted
drawers underneath for our girls. With two more
bedrooms in the house. Merle even added a half bath

up there. This well-done remodel job provided us with much needed space.

Donna and her son Greg (now three), were left in the large downstairs bedroom with two empty bunk beds.

We offered the new room to the rear of the attached garage to those working on the new church being constructed to replace a temporary circus tent used for meetings. A young man named Kit became the first new resident there. He had ventured south from a ministry on the northern coast of California. He moved in and we saw him mostly at dinner as he spent most of his time working on the new church and attending the worship services.

Big risks can be a huge blessing

One evening when he attended church a woman about thirty answered the altar call to give her life to the Lord. She went to a restaurant with Kit and others after the service. This young woman shared her circumstances with the group. Kit was concerned about her and suggested she give me a call me.

When she called the following day, I asked her many questions. She said she needed to get away from her environment and needed a place for her and her three-year-old daughter (Kit had not mentioned a child). This young woman, whose name was Judy, then asked to come over so I could pray with her about her future.

She was using a local phone so she arrived within the hour. She was, a tall thin Italian woman, and wore her dark hair in two pony tails, and she looked striking in a tailored outfit revealing her well-proportioned figure. On her hands were many rings decked with diamonds. Her appearance reflected the fast-pace worldly environment she began to describe to me. As I sought the Lord silently, she revealed the emptiness she felt. Then her eyes filled with tears. I was moved by her sincerity as she talked of her desire to walk the Christian life. She told me her various problems.

She lived close to Los Angeles but far from church. She was employed as a highly paid burlesque dancer and yoga instructor, so she had a very demanding schedule of providing entertainment at the various local bars. To complicate things even more, she felt the urgent need to abandon a damaging relationship with her "live in" boyfriend. When I questioned her about other possible employment, she said her only other job was working as a hair dresser until she found she was allergic the chemicals and even, the rubber gloves used to protect your hands.

Judy was no longer able to cope with her life. She was living with guilt over memories from the recent past. She remembered her husband and older two children crying from the porch of their home begging her not to leave. She left with her youngest in her arms never to return to them again. Her husband had since remarried. Now her life in the fast lane had left her empty, guilt ridden and grief stricken.

Bring them in but not their belongings

We met together as a household and prayed for Judy and her child. The now emptied bunks in Donnas' room were considered for Judy and her daughter to stay. The next day when she called, I offered to let her move in temporarily, only if she were willing to honor the limits we set for her. We offered to move all of her belongings into a storage unit. Only modest clothing could come to our house. The purpose for storing her belongings elsewhere enabled her to leave easily if she so desired. After a couple of weeks if she wanted to stay, she would need to get a job to pay a minimal bed and board fee along with household duty sharing.

After the full day of moving, Judy brought a large armload of clothing and dropped it in the middle of the bedroom. As we sorted through them, it became apparent none of them fit the description of modest. Donna offered to sew pieces into the neck, even add another layer to the micro-mini skirts. These ideas didn't appeal to Judy. Her eyes were on the "Prairie dresses," Donna had sewn and hung in the closet.

Judy attended church nightly. She learned fast by reading the Bible and praying. This house provided the sanctuary she needed to adjust to the Christian life. She started doing her share of the cooking. We were all blessed by her great Italian spaghetti as the aroma of garlic filled the house. We adored her. When she wanted encouragement she would ask, "How am I doing?" Her daughter Immediately became Sheila's constant companion since Janene was in the first grade now and was gone a all day at school. Little Greg and Tracy still played tug of war with the toys. They seemed to enjoy the competition. Merle was restless to move on as he talked more and more of Kansas..

Lord, You said not to condemn the lost. Now I see why! Lord You said,
'"Go and sin no more.

Chapter 19
UPROOTED

And He led them forth by the right way,
that they might go to a city of habitation.
Psalms 107:7

During the summer of 1973 we bought a slide-in camper and truck. Then we took our daughters fishing and camping at various area lakes. We enjoyed our vacations together as a single family. These trips seemed to temporarily satisfy our restlessness to move away.

Donna, Judy, and their kids functioned independently from us. Kit was still working on the new church building along with a roommate Mike.

Merle's work associate Vic began to frequent our house. His wife became gravely ill with terminal cancer and we openly would pray with and for her. These prayers were a comfort to Vic and Doris his wife during these last days they were together

.

Merle recalled a recent conversation between him and this man from his work. Vic would say, "If you ever want to sell your house, be sure to ask me first."

One evening Merle began saying those dreaded statements to me again, "We should move back to Kansas for a while." Then he would qualify his statement with "It would be better for the kids." This subject became more frequent, so I began packing.

Change and then more changes

Born a native Californian, I was a middle child number six of my parents' nine children. I loved living near my brothers and sisters and their families. The very thought of being so far from my parents made me sad. We had made a practice separation when we sold our house in Garden Grove and moved to Oregon for four months. Here in Westminster we had been busily content for nearly three years. Now I had to face the possibility of leaving California again.

I lived among my siblings during their child-bearing years. That was important to me. We had considered ourselves such a close family while we were growing up. My family had no interest in the claims of Christ from the Bible or in churches that evangelize, so this environment here on Cedar Street was extremely unusual to them.

My attempts to explain the Christian beliefs to different ones caused different reactions. One sister attended a prayer meeting with me once in Anaheim. Another let me explain to her the eternal need to agree with God about Jesus Christ and his sacrifice for us on the cross. When I offered her an opportunity to pray she declined. Most of the time our relationships would bounce back from these conversations.

One sister, and her family attended a holiday gathering. She related a story about a group of Christians that had a loud meeting and disturbed the whole neighborhood. This was common for my family to tell negative stories about Christian people they encountered. These stories related in my presence were entertaining to them during family gatherings. Years ago I had told the same stories. Now I silently prayed for the Lord to forgive them. "They don't know you." I didn't feel the need to verbally defend the Christian faith. It seemed to have survived since creation these 6,000 years. I loved my family and I knew God did too. They didn't appear to be open.

On another occasion, this same sister came to visit from Ventura, where she lived. She was recently recovering from a terrific case of spinal meningitis and other difficulties in her life. As she was leaving another sister's house I remembered saying, "I'll pray for you." She placed her hand on her hip, spun to face me, and responded, "Please don't!" I just shrugged my shoulders and said "Ok." My family's rejection of Christ hurt me deeply.

Fifteen years later she became a Christian. She and her husband meet their continuous battles "head on." God is using them now to show us how to stand through great trials and hurts as they pray for their loved ones in need of salvation and healing.

Don't get uptight

I was often hurt when my attempts to share my beliefs with loved family were rejected. At times God just gave me a sense of humor for boldness.

Several years before we had accepted Christ, we frequented another of my sister's homes. She and her husband often played practical jokes on favorite friends in their upper class neighborhood. A neighbor down the block had placed a "For Sale" sign in their yard while they were out of town. This was the style of humor they shared. Now, my brother-in-law was prompted to consider the new basketball goal in this neighbor's yard. This large backstop stuck up high above the block wall fences of the back yards. From my sister's patio door, the back side of this mounting resembled a tall white cross visible clear to the end of the block. I remember laughing at the JESUS SAVES sign placed there to surprise these neighbors when they rounded the corner to return from a stint out of town.

Several years later, after a gathering at my folks' house, this sister and her husband were in their car preparing to leave. I (in fun) stooped down at the car window and thanked them for witnessing to me. They seemed puzzled. "Remember the JESUS SAVES sign?" I joked. "That helped me become a Christian. Thanks for witnessing!" They didn't appear to see the humor in my joke. Often getting on the lighter side was helpful.

Be adventurous trusting God

The suggestions to move became realistic plans. Merle's childhood home of Lawrence appeared to be the best location for us to raise our family. His brother in Kansas offered to employ him as an electrician.

We still had the responsibility of our house, full of furniture and six people living with us. We agreed to call Vic to see if he was still interested in buying our house. To our surprise he was very serious about it and easily agreed on a price we could accept. "Oh, remember the six people that live with us?" Merle added.

Vic said, "Yeah, they can stay. I won't charge them much rent."

Lastly, Merle told him of our plan to take only the belongings that could fit in our small compact car that we would to behind our camper truck. Vic just raised his price on our house to include our furniture, so the residence would be furnished after we left. The Lord was still amazing us with His direct involvement, even in our financial transactions. We had sold our house and furniture and had agreed to let the people remain living there in just fifteen minutes.

Leaving is still hard

How strange it was to open cupboards and drawers and only remove a few special items. The children's belongings took up most of the room. We said our good-bys and headed east to relocate in the bread basket of the Midwest.

> *Lord, how come strangers receive*
> *Your gospel when I tell them?*
> *Yet those that know me reject eternal life.   Oh*
> *yeah! That happened to You.*

Chapter 20
LOSS WITH HOPE

But sanctify the Lord God in your hearts: and be ready always to give an answer to every man that asketh you a reason of the hope that is in you with meekness and fear:

1 Peter 3:15

It had been 20 years since we lived in California. Many amazing events happened after we arrived in Kansas as well, but not lately. It was time for us to be used again, taking examples from those people from the past that were written in our "Book of Remembrance" talked about in the Bible book of Malachi.

We had become complacent. The Bible had become dusty on the bookshelf. Our joy in the Lord and trust in Him had become weak as we neglected reading the Word and praying together. The daily reading in the One Year Bible was a reminder that God's people can be restored to service for Him. "Lord, If You could use us then. You can use us now. We are still Joan and Merle, we are just older. We are thankful to have experiences of witnessing our faith to look back on. Now it's time to go out again."

Settling into our program at the Calvary Chapel Bible College, we became busy with our studies. As we revived our knowledge of God's Word, we quickly became strong with daily devotions, prayer and fellowship.

Interrupted by tragedy

On the tenth day of our student life, we were in class as a messenger interrupted us, asking us to take a phone call upstairs in the office. It is an "Emergency call from Kansas," we were told. When I took the phone, I heard Janene calmly say, "Mom, Scott isn't alive. He got in a wreck in the truck." Sheila was called. Tracy planned to join Janene to deliver the tragic news to Scott's wife, who was pregnant with their third child. Handing the phone to Merle I turned to pastor Bob who was leaning over the lower half of the split door on the office.

In a daze I remember saying, "Scott asked Jesus into his heart. When he had a problem he let us pray with him!" Then I walked away. Knowing Scott's sisters were planning to tell his wife was a painful comfort.

On our way to the apartment that morning, I began to reflect on my first thoughts after hearing of this tragedy. When a loved one leaves this world, all that matters is their relationship to Jesus. There could be no greater gift left behind when we die, than to leave loved ones the confidence that we will see them again.

Remembering Scott

We had always wanted a son. Our girls had little Greg in their midst when they were small. When he and Donna moved on with their lives, our daughters sensed a void in their family order. During the early years Donnas' son Greg had been included in childhood group photos.

By 1982, a series of financial calamities preceded our move into a large old, rented house on Tennessee Street near KU. Merle had become a University of Kansas police officer as we began the succession of compromises that nearly choked our call of service to the Lord. We worked two days during the week as relief parents in a coed group home for adolescents in the organization founded by Dr Karl Menninger.

Our church fellowship was planning a new building as bulletin boards sported pictures of the land and ground-breaking ceremonies. We sang Scripture songs and enjoyed the various Bible studies. During this time our family was unaware God was preparing to place a permanent family member with us.

After years of learning to work in the foster care system, I found my attachment to the social workers became greater than the one I felt for the children that would come and go. This may have been the reason I called Christie that day shortly after our move to Tennessee Street. This social worker had been so patient with me as she taught us to work within the boundaries of the county social work system.

This day A social worker named Christie was too busy to accept a lunch invitation then she said that she had mentioned me as a possible foster care parent for a little boy. I stopped her.

"No, we're not licensing this house for foster care!" Then I asked her, "How old is he?"

This child was small for twelve. His birthday was that week, and he needed a home immediately. He had been abandoned by his father over five years earlier and then left with a couple in a trailer court across town. My series of probing questions revealed he was a student in our daughter Tracy's sixth grade classroom.

The drama of this child entering our lives, was comparable to the events that preceded our biological children: the anticipation of his arrival, the filled, God-given void in our family, and the process of getting to know him.

When Scott was fourteen I picked him up at Circle "C" Ranch (Christian youth camp). He got in my car saying, "I asked Jesus in my heart."

Years later he got married. We prayed with Scott and his wife over concerns. The changes in him after that prayer told us he was beginning to understand his need for Jesus.

"Scott, you had better be careful while driving that big 18 wheeler," I warned. He had told us to be careful in California.

Our son had been so encouraging when he heard we were going to Bible college. He said, "I feel you're doing the right thing." Then we hugged our 24-year-old son for the last time.

Two weeks later, during the funeral, I slipped my hand in my pocket and pulled out a small card given to me by Merle's aunt, Laura Lee. She had handed it to me at an earlier date. When I thanked her she said, "You gave me one like this when I lost my husband. Now I give them out to everyone that is grieving." Lifting this card I began to read a simple poem about "The Weaver" It told of how our lives are but a weaving between we and the Lord. We cannot choose the colors because we are on the ragged underside. When He is done and my loom is silent God will unroll the canvas and explain the reason why the dark treads were as needful in His skillful hand and the threads of Gold and Silver in the pattern He planned for my life.

Keeping the faith through loss

We entered the plane for our return flight to California and our Bible college commitment. Movements seemed mechanical as the ticket process ended with us on the plane by 6:oo am. Merle rolled up his coat to cushion his head against the window. My inventory of the various items in the pocket facing me was only a temporary distraction as I sought to protect myself from thoughts of leaving my loved family again, as well as the extreme distress of the past day's events.

Just before the plane's departure a fair-skinned sun-baked man, probably in his forties, wearing a tailored pressed beige summer suit approached, scanning the numbers printed at his eye level on the luggage compartments. He located his seat on the aisle beside me, sat down and opened the Wall Street Journal with a deep sigh. He looked as if he was doing a routine. Since I was *Sandwiched* between these two men, my curiosity made me wonder about the person on my left.

Allowing him to finish reading before striking up a conversation, I was surprised when he spoke first commenting on the weather, "Glad it didn't snow today! Makes me feel a little safer!"

I began to probe about his plans and traveling experience, knowing he was my captive audience strapped in a seat next to me. He began describing the weather in Australia during his recent safari trip. It appeared he was a man of financial means. He seemed bored with the adventures he described to me, but I would nod or grunt to keep him talking hoping that our conversation could evolve around to satisfy my interest in his spiritual condition. "Wonder what he knows about Jesus Christ?" I pondered.

The time came when he asked me where we were going.

"To Calvary Chapel Bible College in Twin Peaks, California, "I responded. I expected him to be surprised by our age for such a plan as this. I was prepared to give him the story about raising our family in Kansas and then closing our business to enter Bible College. He seemed genuinely interested in our decisions to make such a dramatic change in our life.

Then came the generic response, "I don't talk about religion or politics," he warned. I couldn't let him get away with this. After all, it was my turn to talk. After two hours of conversation, we knew each other fairly well. With a log look at him, I said, "We neglected our Christian faith for many years!" "My son was killed in a wreck last Thursday we're returning from his funeral." The man jolted and shot a glance at me.

"Well, how does THAT make you feel about GOD?"
His tense face revealed eyes of pain.

Startled by this direct statement, I responded calmly, "I don't think it took Him by surprise! Earth isn't a permanent place for any of us!" He seemed to calm with my statement and then studied me. I was unshaken by his harshness. Merle stirred awake, and our conversation converted to introductions. Without his bowing for a sinner's prayer or giving him a Bible, somehow I felt he had been deeply affected by this moment.

"Lord, please send another Christian to touch this man! Have them be patient with him and lovingly continue our conversation to end with his prayer to receive You as his personal Lord and Savior. Amen